Vimal Ghorecha

C# Programming Made Easy. Visual Studio 2008

GRIN Verlag

Bibliografische Information der Deutschen Nationalbibliothek:

Die Deutsche Bibliothek verzeichnet diese Publikation in der Deutschen National-
bibliografie; detaillierte bibliografische Daten sind im Internet über http://dnb.d-
nb.de/ abrufbar.

Imprint:

Copyright © 2013 GRIN Verlag GmbH
Druck und Bindung: Books on Demand GmbH, Norderstedt Germany
ISBN: 978-3-656-67586-0

This book at GRIN:

http://www.grin.com/en/e-book/274606/c-programming-made-easy-visual-studio-
2008

GRIN - Your knowledge has value

Der GRIN Verlag publiziert seit 1998 wissenschaftliche Arbeiten von Studenten, Hochschullehrern und anderen Akademikern als eBook und gedrucktes Buch. Die Verlagswebsite www.grin.com ist die ideale Plattform zur Veröffentlichung von Hausarbeiten, Abschlussarbeiten, wissenschaftlichen Aufsätzen, Dissertationen und Fachbüchern.

Visit us on the internet:

http://www.grin.com/

http://www.facebook.com/grincom

http://www.twitter.com/grin_com

Chapter 1: Introduction to Visual Studio 2008

Introduction to the Visual Studio Development System

Visual Studio 2008 provides advanced development tools, debugging features, database functionality, and innovative features for quickly creating tomorrow's cutting-edge applications across a variety of platforms.

Visual Studio 2008 includes enhancements such as visual designers for faster development with the .NET Framework 3.5, substantial improvements to web development tools and language enhancements that speed development with all types of data. Visual Studio 2008 provides developers with all the tools and framework support required to create compelling, expressive, AJAX-enabled web applications.

Developers will be able to take advantage of these rich client-side and server-side frameworks to easily build client-centric web applications that integrate with any back-end data provider, run within any modern browser and have complete access to ASP.NET application services and the Microsoft platform.

Rapid Application Development

To help developers rapidly create modern software, Visual Studio 2008 delivers improved language and data features, such as Microsoft Language Integrated Query (LINQ), that make it easier for individual programmers to build solutions that analyse and act on information.

Visual Studio 2008 also provides developers with the ability to target multiple versions of the .NET Framework from within the same development environment. Developers will be able to build applications that target the .NET Framework 2.0, 3.0 or 3.5, meaning that they can support a wide variety of projects in the same environment.

Breakthrough User Experience

Visual Studio 2008 offers developers new tools that speed creation of connected applications on the latest platforms including the web, Windows Vista, Office 2007, SQL Server 2008 and Windows Server 2008. For the web, ASP.NET, AJAX and other new technologies will enable developers to quickly create a new generation of more efficient, interactive and personalised web experiences.

Effective Team Collaboration

Visual Studio 2008 delivers expanded and improved offerings that help improve collaboration in development teams, including tools that help integrate database professionals and graphic designers into the development process.

Use the Microsoft .NET Framework 3.5

The .NET Framework enables the rapid construction of connected applications that provide outstanding end-user experiences by providing the building blocks (pre-fabricated software) for solving common programming tasks. Connected applications built on the .NET Framework model business processes effectively and facilitate the integration of systems in heterogeneous environments.

Together Visual Studio and the .NET Framework reduce the need for common plumbing code, reducing development time and enabling developers to concentrate on solving business problems.

C# Programming Made Easy

The .NET Framework 3.5 builds incrementally on the .NET Framework 3.0. Enhancements have been made to feature areas including the base class library, Windows Workflow Foundation, Windows Communication Foundation, Windows Presentation Foundation and Windows CardSpace.

What's New in 2008

- Build applications that use the latest web technologies with improved support for AJAX and web controls and the Microsoft AJAX Library
- Create web applications more easily with an improved design surface and standards support
- Use data from any data source more smoothly with LINQ, a set of language extensions to Visual Basic and Visual C#
- Manage and build applications that target multiple versions of the .NET Framework. For the first time, you can use one tool to work on applications that run on .NET Framework versions 2.0, 3.0, and 3.5
- Ensure application correctness more easily with integrated unit testing in Visual Studio 2008 Professional Edition
- Discover the full power of the .NET Framework 3.5 with integrated tools that simplify building great user experiences and connected systems
- Build stunning user experiences with integrated designers for Windows Presentation Foundation. Experiences built with Windows Presentation Foundation can interoperate seamlessly with Windows Forms
- Create connected applications using new visual designers for Windows Communications Foundation and Windows Workflow Foundation
- Use Visual Studio's professional development environment to build Microsoft Office-based solutions that are reliable, scalable and easy to maintain (available in Visual Studio 2008 Professional Edition only)
- Enhance collaboration between developers and designers to create more compelling user experiences

Feature Highlights

- Build applications for Windows, the web, the Microsoft Office system, the .NET Framework, SQL Server and Windows Mobile with integrated drag-and-drop designers
- Visual Studio integrates Visual Basic, Visual C# and Visual C++ to support a wide variety of development styles
- Editor features such as Edit and Continue and Microsoft IntelliSense simplify the cycle of designing, developing and debugging an application
- Deploy client applications easily with ClickOnce, which enables developers and IT pros to deploy an application and its prerequisites and then ensure that the application remains up-to-date
- Build applications which target the .NET Framework, shortening development time by reducing the need for infrastructure code and helping to enhance application security
- Use ASP.NET to speed the creation of interactive, highly appealing web applications and web services. Master Pages allow developers to easily manage a consistent site layout in one place
- A community of millions of developers ensures that developers can find partners and other community members addressing the same challenges

Visual Studio Editions with Features

Visual Studio is available in several editions: Standard, Professional, Tools for Office, and Team System.

The core languages included with Visual Studio — Visual Basic, Visual C++, Visual C#, and Visual J# — as well as Visual Web Developer are each also offered in separate Express editions.

C# Programming Made Easy

The following table lists the different features and tools available with Express editions, Visual Studio Standard and Professional editions, and Visual Studio Tools for Office.

Feature	Express	Standard	Professional	Visual Studio Tools for Office
Programming languages included	Visual Basic, Visual C#, Visual C++, and Visual J# are single language. Visual Web Developer includes Visual C# and Visual Basic.	All	All	Visual Basic and Visual C# only.
User experience	Simplified menu options and defaults	Simplified menu options and defaults	Full	Full
Documentation	10mb "Getting Started"; Starter Kits targeted at first-time programmers 200mb optional MSDN Express	Full MSDN Library	Full MSDN Library	Full MSDN Library
IntelliSense	Yes	Yes	Yes	Yes
Code editor	Yes	Yes	Yes	Yes
Code snippets	Yes	Yes	Yes	Yes
Windows Forms designer	Not available with Visual Web Developer	Yes	Yes	Yes
Web Forms designer	Only available with Visual Web Developer	Yes	Yes	Yes
Mobile Device support	No	Yes	Yes	No
Database design tools to create and modify tables and stored procedures	Local only	Local and remote	Local and remote	Local and remote
Data access designers	Visual Basic, Visual C#, Visual C++, local only. Visual Web Developer includes local and remote.	Local and remote	Local and remote	Local and remote

Class Designer	No	Yes	Yes	Yes
Object Test Bench	No	Yes	Yes	Yes
XML editor support	XML editing available. Basic XSLT support available only with Visual Web Developer	Full XML and XSLT	Full XML and XSLT	Full XML and XSLT
Deployment tools	ClickOnce only	ClickOnce only	All tools	All tools
Extensibility	Add external tools to the menu only. Use 3rd party controls.	Consume extensions	Full	Full
Server Explorer Servers node	No	No	Yes	No
Reporting	SQL Server Reporting Services Add-in available with Visual Web Developer only	SQL Server Reporting Services	SQL Server Reporting Services and Crystal Reports	SQL Server Reporting Services
Source Code Control	No	MSSCCI-compatible (Visual SourceSafe sold separately)	MSSCCI-compatible (Visual SourceSafe sold separately)	MSSCCI-compatible (Visual SourceSafe sold separately)
Local debugging	Yes	Yes	Yes	Yes
Remote debugging	No	No	Yes	No
SQL Server 2005 integration	No	No	Yes	Yes
SQL Server 2005 Editions	SQL Server 2005 Express Edition	SQL Server 2005 Express Edition	SQL Server 2005 Developer Edition	SQL Server 2005 Developer Edition

Introduction to the IDE (Visual C#)

The Visual C# integrated development environment (IDE) is a collection of development tools exposed through a common user interface. Some of the tools are shared with other Visual Studio languages, and some, such as the C# compiler, are unique to Visual C#. The documentation in this section provides an overview of how to use the most important Visual C# tools as you work in the IDE in various phases of the development process.

The following are the most important tools and windows in Visual C#. The windows for most of these tools can be opened from the **View** menu.

- The Code Editor, for writing source code.
- The C# compiler, for converting C# source code into an executable program.
- The Visual Studio debugger, for testing your program.
- The **Toolbox** and **Designer**, for rapid development of user interfaces using the mouse.
- **Solution Explorer**, for viewing and managing project files and settings.
- **Project Designer**, for configuring compiler options, deployment paths, resources, and more.
- **Class View**, for navigating through source code according to types, not files.
- **Properties Window**, for configuring properties and events on controls in your user interface.
- Object Browser, for viewing the methods and classes available in dynamic link libraries including .NET Framework assemblies and COM objects.
- Document Explorer, for browsing and searching product documentation on your local machine and on the Internet.

How the IDE Exposes the Tools

You interact with the tools through windows, menus, property pages, and wizards in the IDE. The basic IDE looks something like this:

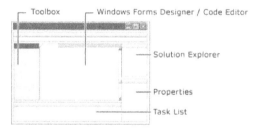

You can quickly access any open tool windows or files by pressing CTRL + TAB.

Editor and Windows Form Designer Windows

The large main window is used by both the Code Editor and the Windows Forms Designer. You can toggle between code view and Design view by pressing F7, or clicking **Code** or **Designer** on the **View** menu. While in Design view, you can drag controls onto the window from the **Toolbox**, which you can make visible by clicking on the **Toolbox** tab on the left margin.

The **Properties** window in the lower right is populated only in Design view. It enables you to set properties and hook up events for user interface controls such as buttons, text boxes, and so on. When you set this window to **Auto Hide**, it will collapse into the right margin whenever you switch to **Code View**.

Solution Explorer and Project Designer

The window in the top right is **Solution Explorer**, which shows all the files in your project in a hierarchical tree view. When you use the **Project** menu to add new files to your project, you will see them reflected in **Solution Explorer**. In addition to files, **Solution Explorer** also displays your project settings, and references to external libraries required by your application.

The **Project Designer** property pages are accessed by right-clicking on the **Properties** node in **Solution Explorer**, and then clicking **Open**. Use these pages to modify build options, security requirements, deployment details, and many other project properties

Compiler, Debugger, and Error List Windows

The C# compiler has no window because it is not an interactive tool, but you can set compiler options in the **Project Designer**. When you click **Build** on the **Build** menu, the C# compiler is invoked by the IDE. If the build is successful, the status pane displays a Build Succeeded message. If there were build errors, the **Error List** window appears below the editor/designer window with a list of errors. Double-click an error to go to the problem line in your source code. Press F1 to see Help documentation for the highlighted error.

The debugger has various windows that display values of variables and type information as your application is running. You can use the Code Editor window while debugging to specify a line at which to pause execution in the debugger, and to step through code one line at a time.

Customizing the IDE

All of the windows in Visual C# can be made dockable or floating, hidden or visible, or can be moved to new locations. To change the behavior of a window, click the down arrow or push-pin icons on the title bar and select from among the available options. To move a docked window to a new docked location, drag the title bar until the window dropper icons appear. While holding down the left mouse button, move the mouse pointer over the icon at the new location. Position the pointer over the left, right, top or bottom icons to dock the window on the specified side. Position the pointer over the middle icon to make the window a tabbed window. As you position the pointer, a blue semi-transparent rectangle appears, which indicates where the window will be docked in the new location.

Following are different templates under Project Types and their use.

Windows Application:
> This template allows to create standard windows based applications. Windows Applications are form based standard Windows desktop applications for common day to day tasks. (Ex: Microsoft word).

Class Library:
> Class libraries are those that provide functionality similar to Active X and DLL by creating classes that access other applications. Class library contains components and libraries to

be used inside other applications. A Class library can not be executed and thus it does not have any entry point.

Windows Control Library:

This allows to create our own windows controls. Also called as User Controls, where you group some controls, add it to the toolbox and make it available to other projects. Windows Control Library contains user defined windows controls to be used by Windows applications.

Web Application:

This allows to create web-based applications using IIS. We can create web pages, rich web applications and web services. Web applications are programs that used to run inside some web server (Ex:IIS) to fulfill the user requests over the http. (Ex: Hotmail and Google).

Web Service:

Allows to create XML Web Services. Web services are web applications that provide services to other applications over the internet.

Web Control Library:

Allows to create User-defined controls for the Web. Similar to user defined windows controls but these are used for Web. Web Control Library contains user defined web controls to be used by web applications.

Console Application:

A new kind of application in Visual Studio .NET. They are command line based applications. Console applications are light weight programs run inside the command prompt (DOS) window. They are commonly used for test applications.

Windows Service:

These run continuously regardless of the user interaction. They are designed for special purpose and once written, will keep running and come to an end only when the system is shut down.

Other:

This template is to develop other kinds of applications like enterprise applications, database applications etc.

❖ .NET Framework & Architecture

Microsoft .NET supports not only language independence, but also language integration. This means that you can take the advantage of classes, inheritance of classes etc. across different languages. The **.NET Framework** makes this possible with a specification called the **Common Type System (CTS)** that all .NET components must follow. The term .Net Framework refers to the group of technologies that form the development environment for the Microsoft .Net platform.

It also includes a **Common Language Specification (CLS)**, which provides a series of basic rules that are required for language integration. The CLS determines the minimum requirements for being a .NET language. Compilers that conform to the CLS create objects that can interoperate with one another. The entire Framework Class Library (FCL) can be used by any language that conforms to the CLS.

The .NET Framework sits on top of the operating system, which can be any flavor of Windows from Win 98 forward, and consists of a number of components.

The .NET Framework consists of:

- Different languages: VB.NET, C#, J#, and JScript .NET
- The **Common Language Runtime**, an object-oriented platform for Windows and web development that all these languages share
- A number of related class libraries, collectively known as the Framework Class Library (FCL) (BCL).

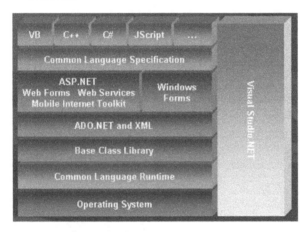

The most important component of the .NET Framework is the CLR, which provides the environment in which programs are executed. The CLR includes a virtual machine. At a high level, the CLR activates objects, performs security checks on them, store them out in memory, executes them, and garbage-collects them. The Common Type System is also part of the CLR.

The layer on top of the CLR is a set of framework base classes (BCL), followed by an additional layer of data and XML classes, plus another layer of classes intended for web services, Web Forms, and Windows Forms. Collectively, these classes are known as the Framework Class

Library, one of the largest class libraries in history and one that provides an object-oriented API to all the functionality that the .NET platform encapsulates. With more than 4,000 classes, the FCL facilitates rapid development of desktop, client/server, and other web services and applications.

Web Forms and Windows Forms allow you to apply Rapid Application Development techniques to building web and Windows applications. Simply drag and drop controls onto your form, double-click a control, and write the code to respond to the associated event.

❖ Features of .NET Platform

The core component of the .NET platform is found in the Common Language Runtime, Base Class Library & the Common Language Specification. The .NET BCL expose the features of the CLR in much the same way that the Windows API allows you to utilize the features of the Windows operating system; however, it also provides many higher-level features that facilitate code reuse.

This architecture gives a great number of benefits, not the least of which is a consistent API. By writing to the CLR & using the .NET BCL, all application services are available via a common object oriented programming model.

The new programming model greatly simplifies the efforts that were required when writing Windows DNA applications or fir that matter, almost Win32 & OM project.

Another great benefit for .NET benefit for .NET developers is its model for error handling via exceptions.

In .NET all errors are reported via exceptions, which greatly simplify writing, reading, & maintaining code. Thanks to Common Language Specification & Common Type System, .NET exception work across module & language boundaries.

1) Multilanguage Development:

Different types of application and programmer required to work with different types of programming languages. With the use of CLR the component of .Net framework, it is easy to work with different types of languages in .net platform. In .Net platform programmers can choose the languages which best for them. Additionally, .Net framework allows the integration of these different languages through the use of MSIL. Currently .Net supports languages like VB.Net, C#.net, J#.Net, Jscript.Net, COBOL, Fortran, Perl, Python and many more. In .Net platform, we can develop different types of application like windows, web or portable application which runs on PDA or mobile device.

2) Platform and Processor Independence

When we compile any application in .Net platform first it converted into MSIL code. This MSIL code is CPU-Independent and is higher then any machine language. After creation of MSIL code, this code can be run on any platform and processor which supports Common Language Runtime. So, programmers can develop application which can be run on any platform and processor.

3) Automatic Memory Management:

The programmers always worry about the Memory while it is developing any type of application. We already use, program like C and C++, we are allocating memory to particular object using different function and we release this memory when program is terminated. In .Net environment, Microsoft is provide facility to make developing easier. It provide a component called Garbage Collection which handles this memory management task. When any object required memory it automatically allocates it and when that is no longer valid then it automatically free up those memory to resue.

4) Easy Deploying:

After developing any type of application, programmers always worry about how they can deploy (install) their application. Most of the companies use third party software to build their installation. These installation contain a large number of files installed in different directory, various registry setting required, COM componets and short cuts may required. The .Net application doesn't require any extra activity than copying their files to a directory. For uninstalling an application will be easy as deleting those files. This is because .Net components are not referenced in registry because of Metadata.

5) Distributed Architecture:

Today, application or websites which are presented to user come from different sources like servers located at different places and different application running on this server which fetches data from many database. This called distributed architecture. This type of application are very complex to build and maintain. Each interface uses different types of programming concept to fetch data. The .Net provide architecture for developing this type of complex application using different concept like XML, SOAP, UDDI.

6) Interoperability with Unmanaged Code:

The code which is generated by CLR are is known as managed code. So, code outside from CLR and not managed by CLR is unmanaged code. However, this code is still run by the CLR but we cant take the advantage like CTS and automatic memory management. There are many situation arrive, when you have to work with code that is outside from .Net platform. Companies doesn't deliver a .Net component version of their products every time. So, Microsoft add a functionality in CLR so it can work with this unmanaged code. Examples of unmanaged code are calling DLL files, Calling COM components.

7) Security:

Distributed component application require security. The .Net designer follow the approach which provides separation and access control based on user account. Security for .Net applications starts as soon as a class is loaded by the CLR. Before the class is loaded, the accessibility rules and requirement are checked. Additionally, when code request, access to the certain resources, the class identification are verified.

8) Performance and Scalability:

There is no magic tool that will allow a poorly designed application to scale and perform well. The .Net framework gives you a tools that make it easier to design better performing software.

❖ Components of .NET Architecture

Following are the different components of .Net Architecture. Each explain in detail with their functionality.

1) .Net Runtime (Common Language Runtime):

The heart of the .Net framework is the CLR. This is similar to the Java Virtual Machine. It is an environment that executes MSIL code. In java, the JVM is the concept of one language for all purpose while .Net platform supports multiple programming languages through the use of Common Language Specification. It is also referred to as a managed environment, one in which common services, such as garbage collection and security, are automatically provided. Following are the different feature provided by

Process of compilation and executing:

Code that we have develop with language compiler and run under the CLR is called managed code. It provides the functionality like cross-language integration, exception handling, security. To provide services to managed code, language compiler are required to add metadata with it. It means they provide information that describes the types, members and reference used in code. Metadata is stored with code. When class loader loads the code, it uses the metadata to locate and load classes, allocate required memory, solve method invocation, generate native code, apply security and set up run time boundaries for application.

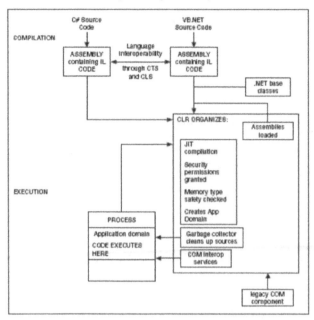

2) Managed and Unmanaged Code:

Managed Code is what Visual Basic .NET and C# compilers create. It compiles to Intermediate Language (IL), not to machine code that could run directly on your computer. The IL is kept in a file called an assembly, along with metadata that describes the classes, methods, and attributes (such as security requirements) of the code you've created. This assembly is the one-stop-shopping unit of deployment in the .NET world. You copy it to another server to deploy the assembly there—and often that copying is the only step required in the deployment.

Managed code runs in the Common Language Runtime. The runtime offers a wide variety of services to your running code. In the usual course of events, it first loads and verifies the assembly to make sure the IL is okay. Then, just in time, as methods are called, the runtime arranges for them to be compiled to machine code suitable for the machine the assembly is running on, and caches this machine code to be used the next time the method is called. As the assembly runs, the runtime continues to provide services such as security, memory management, threading, and the like.

Unmanaged code is what you use to make before Visual Studio .NET was released. Visual Basic 6, Visual C++ 6, heck, even that 15-year old C compiler you may still have kicking around on your hard drive all produced unmanaged code. It compiled directly to machine code that run on the machine where you compiled it and on other machines as long as they had the same chip, or nearly the same.

It didn't get services such as security or memory management from an invisible runtime; it got them from the operating system. And importantly, it got them from the operating system explicitly, by asking for them, usually by calling an API provided in the Windows

3) Intermediate Language:

MSIL is the CPU-independent instruction set into which .Net framework programs are compiled. It contains instructions for loading, storing, initializing and calling method of different objects. MSIL contains code and Metadata which is true cross language integration. It is also known as CIL (common intermediate language) or IL (intermediate language). We can directly code into MSIL language but it is rare case.

4) Common Type System:

As Microsoft .Net provide application development using different programming languages. For this, Microsoft has provided Common Type System which means we don't have to worry when we are developing multiple languages about how a data types declared in one language needs to be declared in another. Any .Net type has the same attributes regardless of the language it is used in. In .Net all data types are objects which derived from System. Object. So, all data types derive from a common base class, they all share some basic functionality.

5) Base Class Library:

In C and C++, we include header files like stdio.h, conio.h for using library functions. In .NET, BCL, is the collection of classes and namespaces which we use in application for variety of inbuilt functionality. The .NET framework Base Class Library provides an extensive collection of classes which are hierarchically organized via namespaces. This library consists of classes related to Data, XML, Web Forms, Windows Form, Smart Device, Input Output etc.

The namespace is logical container or partition which group the different classes related to same functionality. It looks like drive's or folder in our computer. We organized our data into different folders or drives. For specific information or files we go into the specific folder or drive for faster retrieval of information.

The root of the hierarchy of Base Class Library is System namespace. Here, two classes can have same name but they must reside in different namespace. Following are the listing of some common namespace with its description.

Namespace	Contains
System	Fundamental and base classes that defines commonly used value and references data types, events, interface, attributes
System.Data	Classes related to ADO.NET which useful for working with database
System.Collections	Classes used for various objects like lists, queue, array etc.

System.Drawing	Classes related to GUI drawings
System.IO	Classes related to reading and writing data streams and files
System.Web.UI	Classes related to create controls and pages that will appear on Web applications as user interface on a web page.
System.Windows.Form	Classes for creating Windows-based applications that take full advantage of rich user interface
System.XML	Provide standards-based support for processing XML.

6) Assemblies:

Assemblies are the building blocks of .NET Framework applications; they form the fundamental unit of deployment, version control, reuse, activation scoping, and security permissions. An assembly is a collection of types and resources that are built to work together and form a logical unit of functionality. An assembly provides the common language runtime with the information it needs to be aware of type implementations.

It contains code that the common language runtime executes. Microsoft intermediate language (MSIL) code in a portable executable (PE) file will not be executed if it does not have an associated assembly metadata.

Assemblies can be static or dynamic. Static assemblies can include .NET Framework types (interfaces and classes), as well as resources for the assembly (bitmaps, JPEG files, resource files, and so on). Static assemblies are stored on disk in portable executable (PE) files. You can also use the .NET Framework to create dynamic assemblies, which are run directly from memory and are not saved to disk before execution. A static assembly can consist of four elements: Assembly metadata, Type metadata, Microsoft intermediate language (MSIL) code that implements the types, A set of resources.
A private assembly is used by a single application and is store in that application's install directory. A shared assembly is one that can be referenced by more than one application.

7) Metadata:

The data about data is called Metadata. It is a feature that lets the CLR know the details about a particular component or object. The metadata for an object is persisted at compiled time and then queried at runtime so that the CLR know how to initialize object, call their methods and access their properties. An application can interrogate metadata and learn what an object exposes. This process is known as **reflection.** This data is stored in component itself in a binary format inside an assembly. It contains a declaration for every type including names and its members like methods, fields, properties and event. When a class loader of CLR loads an assembly at that time it uses a metadata to locate the body of method.

8) Assembly Cache:

The assembly cache is a directory which contains the different assembly on the machine. There are two types of assembly cache: A global assembly cache and a transient (temporary) assembly cache.

When assemblies are downloaded to the local machine using browser, it is automatically installed in the transient assembly cache. Each computer where the common language runtime is installed has a machine-wide code cache called the global assembly cache. The global assembly cache stores assemblies specifically designated to be shared by several applications on the computer.

You should share assemblies by installing them into the global assembly cache only when you need to. As a general guideline, keep assembly dependencies private, and locate assemblies in the application directory unless sharing an assembly is explicitly required.

9) Reflection:

Reflection is the process by which .NET applications can access an assembly's metadata information and discover its methods and data types at runtime. We can also dynamically invoke methods and use type information through late binding through Reflection API. System.type class is the core of the reflection. It is used to represent a Common Type System which includes methods that allow to determined type's name, which module it contain and its namespace with it contains value or reference type.

Using System.Reflection.Assembly class you can retrieve all of the types in an assembly and all modules contained in the assembly. To invoke any method of class named Activator class to create instance and then GetMethod method to invoke the method.

10)   Just-In-Time Compilation (JIT):

When any .NET application compile, it is not converted into machine code but it converted into MSIL (Intermediate Code). This code is machine independent. So, CLR provide Just In Time compilation technology to convert the MSIL code into a platform/device-specific code so that it can be executed.

The .NET provide three types of JIT compilers:

Pre-JIT: This JIT compiles an assembly's entire code into native code at one cycle. Normally, it is used at installation time.

Econo-JIT: This compiler is used on devices with limited resources. It compiles the IL code bit-by-bit freeing resources used by the cached native code when required.

Normal-JIT: The default JIT compiles code only as it is called and places the resulting native code in the cache.

When, JIT compiles, the native code is placed into the cache, so that when the next call is made to the same method, the cached code is executed. So it increase the application speed.

11) Garbage Collection:

Memory management is one of the housekeeping duty that takes a lot of programming time in developing application. We doesn't like spent a time for programming related to memory. So .NET provides a environment with the garbage collection system. Garbage collection runs when application needs free memory. There is no exact time of execution of garbage collection system.

When application required more memory and the memory allocator reports that there is no free memory than garbage collection is called. It start by assuming that everything should be deleted from the memory. First it create a graph of used memory by application. When it has complete graph of memory used by application then it copies this data and free up the whole memory. And reallocate the memory to the application.

Garbage collector also free up the memory for unused object at regular interval. We do not have to write code to perform memory management task when developing managed applications

❖ Explain CTS, CLR and JIT

CLR (Common Language Runtime):-   The most important concept of the .net framework is the existence and functionality of the .net common language runtime (CLR), also called .net runtime and short. It is a framework layer that resides above the OS and handles the execution of all the .net applications. Our programs don't directly communicate with the OS but go through the CLR.

CTS (Common Type System):- .NET also defines a common type system (CTS). Like CLS, CTS is also a set of standards. CTS defines the basic data types that IL understands. Each .Net compliant language should map its data types to these standard data types. This makes it possible for the 2 languages to communicate with each other by passing/receiving parameters to and from each other. For example, CTS defines a type, int32, an integral data type of 32 bits(4 bytes) which is mapped by C# through int and VB.net through its integer data type.

JIT (Just In Time Compilers):- When out IL compiled code needs to be executed, the CLR invokes the JIT compiler, which compile the IL code to native executable code(.exe of .dll) that is designed for specific machine and OS. JITers in many ways are different from traditional compliers as they compile the IL to native code JIT. So, the part of code that is not used by that particular run is never converted to native code. If some IL code is converted to native code, then the next time it's needed, the CLR reuses the same (already compiled) copy without re-compiling. So, if a program runs for some time (assuming that all or most of the functions get called). Then it won't have any just-in-time performance penalty.

As JITers are aware of the specific processor and OS at runtime and OS at runtime. They can optimize the code extremely efficiently resulting in very robust applications. Also, since a JIT compiler knows the exact current state of executable code. They can also optimize the code by in-lining small function calls (like replacing body of small function when its called in a loop, saving the function call time). Although Microsoft stated that C# and .net are not competing with language like C++ in efficiency and speed of execution. JITers can makes your code even faster than C++ code in some cases when the program in run over an extended period of time.

❖ Managed Vs. Unmanaged Code

Manage code: -

The execution of manage code is done by following steps.

1. Selecting language complier.
2. Completing the code to IL (information language).
3. Completing IL to native code.
4. Executing code.

The CLR is used by selecting one or more language complier such as VB, C++, VC++, java, JavaScript etc. The language complier will decide the syntax of the code. When the program is compile then that code is called manage code. The complier will convert the source code to IL which is dependent on CPU. Just in time complier converts IL into native or CPU specific code. When you compile source code to IL required metadata is generated.

Unmanaged Code:-

The unmanaged code directly complies with the mechanic code and executed when a work it is complete. It does not have services such as security and memory management but the OS is gives this services at runtime. The OS gives these services by calling the API of the window.

❖ Explain Assemblies and Metadata

Meta data describes source code or program which is in binary information stored in CLR portable executable file or in the memory. When the compilation when the code take place in DE file then metadata in inserted in the file. The metadata describes data types and members used in the program. When the code is executed the CLR loads the metadata into the memory and finds information about classes and its members.

Meta Data Contains:-

Assembly information such as name, version, type of assembly, reference assembly and security permission. Information about type such as name, interfaces used, methods, fields, properties, events based class etc. It maintains attributes information which are modified by the user.

Assemblies:-

The assembly contains code which is executed by CLR (Common Language Runtime). There are two types of assembly.

1. Dynamic:- Dynamic assembly will run directly from the memory without saving but it can be saved after execution.

2. Static:- Static assembly includes interfaces classes and resources. This assembly are stored in PE files.

Assembly Contains:-

Assembly in a logical unit which consist of four parts.

1. Manifest:-

2. Type Metadata

Every assembly, whether static or dynamic, contains a collection of data that describes how the elements in the assembly relate to each other. The assembly manifest contains this assembly metadata. An assembly manifest contains all the metadata needed to specify the assembly's version requirements and security identity, and all metadata needed to define the scope of the assembly and resolve references to resources and classes. The assembly manifest can be stored in either a PE file (an .exe or .dll) with Microsoft intermediate language (MSIL) code or in a standalone PE file that contains only assembly manifest information. It contains Assembly name, Version number, Culture, Strong name information, List of all files in the assembly, Type reference information, Information on referenced assemblies.

Type Metadata is information stored in the assembly that describes the types and methods of the assembly and provides other useful information about the assembly. Assemblies are said to be self-describing because the metadata fully describes the contents of each module

❖ **Managed execution process of .NET applications.**

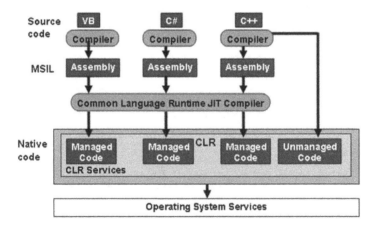

The process of executing .NET application is divided into different steps. First steps is select a compiler based on language which you have written source code. There are different compiler available in .NET framework like for VB.NET select VBC, for C# select CSC etc.

In, second step the source code is converted into MSIL code which contains assembly and metadata information.

Next step, the MSIL code is translated into native code by using CLR's JIT compiler. In final step of execution, the CLR provides environments which run this native code on machine and provides other related services.

❖ Namespace

The **namespace** keyword is used to declare a scope. This namespace scope lets you organize code and gives you a way to create globally unique types. Even if you do not explicitly declare one, a default namespace is created. This unnamed namespace, sometimes called the global namespace, is present in every file. Any identifier in the global namespace is available for use in a named namespace. Namespaces implicitly have public access and this is not modifiable.

The Namespace Hierarchy and Fully-Qualified Names

You're probably already familiar with namespaces from the .NET Framework Class Library. For example, the Button type is contained in the System.Windows.Forms namespace. That's actually shorthand for the situation shown in Figure 2, shows that the Button class is contained in the Forms namespace that is ontained in the Windows namespace that is contained in the root System namespace.

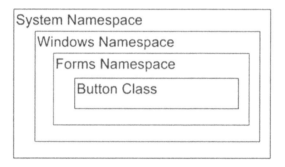

Figure 2. A namespace and class hierarchy

The fully qualified name of a class is constructed by concatenating the names of all the namespaces that contain the type. For example, the fully qualified name of the Button class is System.Windows.Forms.Button. The namespace hierarchy helps distinguish types with the same name from one another. For example, you might define your own class named Button, but it might be contained in the ControlPanel Namespace within the PowerPlant namespace, making its fully qualified name PowerPlant.ControlPanel.Button.

Declaring Namespaces

You can use the Namespace statement to declare a namespace in your own code. Namespace statements can be nested. For example, a C# .NET module could contain these lines of code:

Namespace PowerPlant

{

    Namespace ControlPanel

    {

        Public Class Button

        {

            ' Statements to implement Button

        }

    }

}

An alternative way to express this same hierarchy is to combine the Namespace statements:

Namespace PowerPlant.ControlPanel

{

    Public Class Button

    {

        ' Statements to implement Button

    }

}

By default, a C# .NET project declares a *root namespace* that has the same name as the project. If the above declaration was in a project called PowerLib, then the fully qualified name of the Button class would be PowerLib.PowerPlant.ControlPanel.Button. You can change the name of the root namespace by following these steps:

1. In Project Explorer, right-click the project and select **Properties**.
2. Click **Common Properties**.
3. Enter a new name for the Root Namespace. It's good practice to use a name such as **CompanyName.Technology** for the Root Namespace, to avoid conflicts with namespaces defined by other developers.
4. Click **OK**.

Note Strictly speaking, assemblies and namespaces are orthogonal. That is, you can declare members of a single namespace across multiple assemblies, or declare multiple namespaces in a single assembly. Unless you have a good reason for such an arrangement, though, it's best to keep things simple with one namespace per assembly and vice versa

The using Directive

Obviously, namespaces can grow rather long and tiresome to type, and the ability to indicate a particular class with such specificity may not always be necessary. Fortunately, C# allows you to abbreviate a class's full name. To do this, list the class's namespace at the top of the file, prefixed with the using keyword. Throughout the rest of the file, you can refer to the types in the namespace simply by their type names:

```
using System;
using Wrox.ProCSharp;
```

As remarked earlier, virtually all C# source code will have the statement using System; simply because so many useful classes supplied by Microsoft are contained in the System namespace.

If two namespaces referenced by using statements contain a type of the same name, you will need to use the full (or at least a longer) form of the name to ensure that the compiler knows which type is
to be accessed. For example, say classes called NamespaceExample exist in both the Wrox.ProCSharp
.Basics and Wrox.ProCSharp.OOP namespaces. If you then create a class called Test in the Wrox.ProCSharp namespace, and instantiate one of the NamespaceExample classes in this class, you need to specify which of these two classes you're talking about:

```
using Wrox.ProCSharp;

class Test
{
    public static int Main()
    {
        Basics.NamespaceExample nSEx = new Basics.NamespaceExample();
       // do something with the nSEx variable.
        return 0;
    }
}
```

Because using *statements occur at the top of C# files, in the same place that C and C++ list #include statements, it's easy for programmers moving from C++ to C# to confuse namespaces with C++-style header files. Don't make this mistake. The* using *statement does no physical linking between files, and C# has no equivalent to C++ header files.*

Your organization will probably want to spend some time developing a namespace schema so that its developers can quickly locate functionality that they need and so that the names of the organization's homegrown classes won't conflict with those in off-the-shelf class libraries.

Namespace Aliases

Another use of the using keyword is to assign aliases to classes and namespaces. If you have a very long namespace name that you want to refer to several times in your code but don't want to include in a simple using statement (for example, to avoid type name conflicts), you can assign an alias to the namespace. The syntax for this is:

using alias = NamespaceName;

The following example (a modified version of the previous example) assigns the alias Introduction to the Wrox.ProCSharp.Basics namespace and uses this to instantiate a NamespaceExample object, which is defined in this namespace. Notice the use of the namespace alias qualifier (::). This forces the search to start with the Introduction namespace alias. If a class called Introduction had been introduced in the same scope, a conflict would happen. The :: operator allows the alias to be referenced even if the conflict exists. The NamespaceExample class has one method, GetNamespace(), which uses the GetType() method exposed by every class to access a Type object representing the class's type. You use this object to return a name of the class's namespace:

```
using System;
using Introduction = Wrox.ProCSharp.Basics; class
Test
{
    public static int Main()
    {
        Introduction::NamespaceExample        NSEx        =        new
Introduction::NamespaceExample();
        Console.WriteLine(NSEx.GetNamespace());
        return 0;
    }
}

namespace Wrox.ProCSharp.Basics
{
    class NamespaceExample
    {
        public string GetNamespace()
        {
            return this.GetType().Namespace;
        }
    }
}
```

The Main() Method

C# programs start execution at a method named Main(). This must be a static method of a class (or struct), and must have a return type of either int or void.

Although it is common to specify the public modifier explicitly, because by definition the method must be called from outside the program, it doesn't actually matter what accessibility level you assign to the entry-point method — it will run even if you mark the method as private.

Multiple Main() Methods

When a C# console or Windows application is compiled, by default the compiler looks for exactly one Main() method in any class matching the signature that was just described and makes that class method the entry point for the program. If there is more than one Main() method, the compiler will return an error message. For example, consider the following code called MainExample.cs:

```
using System;

namespace Wrox.ProCSharp.Basics
{
    class Client
    {
        public static int Main()
        {
            MathExample.Main();
            return 0;
        }
    }

    class MathExample
    {
        static int Add(int x, int y)
        {
            return x + y;
        }

        public static int Main()
        {
            int i = Add(5,10);
            Console.WriteLine(i);
            return 0;
        }
    }
}
```

This contains two classes, both of which have a Main() method. If you try to compile this code in the usual way, you will get the following errors:

csc MainExample.cs

Microsoft (R) Visual C# Compiler version 9.00.20404 for
Microsoft (R) .NET Framework version 3.5
Copyright (C) Microsoft Corporation. All rights reserved.

MainExample.cs(7,23): error CS0017: Program 'MainExample.exe' has more than
one entry point defined: 'Wrox.ProCSharp.Basics.Client.Main()'
MainExample.cs(21,23): error CS0017: Program 'MainExample.exe' has more
than one entry point defined: 'Wrox.ProCSharp.Basics.MathExample.Main()'

However, you can explicitly tell the compiler which of these methods to use as the entry
point for the program by using the /main switch, together with the full name (including
namespace) of the class to which the Main() method belongs:

csc MainExample.cs /main:Wrox.ProCSharp.Basics.MathExample

Passing Arguments to Main()

The examples so far have shown only the Main() method without any parameters. However,
when the program is invoked, you can get the CLR to pass any command-line arguments to
the program by including a parameter. This parameter is a string array, traditionally called
args (although C# will accept any name). The program can use this array to access any
options passed through the command line when the program is started.

The following sample, ArgsExample.cs, loops through the string array passed in to the Main()
method and writes the value of each option to the console window:

```
using System;

namespace Wrox.ProCSharp.Basics
{
    class ArgsExample
    {
        public static int Main(string[] args)
        {
            for (int i = 0; i < args.Length; i++)
            {
                Console.WriteLine(args[i]);
            }
            return 0;
        }
    }
}
```

Your First C# Program

Let's start by compiling and running the simplest possible C# program — a simple class consisting of a console application that writes a message to the screen.

The Code

Type the following into a text editor (such as Notepad), and save it with a .cs extension (for example, First.cs). The Main() method is shown here:

```
using  System;

namespace  Wrox.ProCSharp.Basics
{
    class  MyFirstCSharpClass
    {
        static  void  Main()
        {
            Console.WriteLine("This isn't at all like Java!");
            Console.ReadLine();
            return;
        }
    }
}
```

Compiling and Running the Program

You can compile this program by simply running the C# command-line compiler (csc.exe) against the source file, like this:

```
csc  First.cs
```

If you want to compile code from the command line using the csc command, you should be aware that the .NET command-line tools, including csc, are available only if certain environment variables have been set up. Depending on how you installed .NET (and Visual Studio 2008), this may or may not be the case on your machine.

Compiling the code produces an executable file named First.exe, which you can run from the command line or from Windows Explorer like any other executable. Give it a try:

csc First.cs

```
Microsoft (R) Visual C# Compiler version 9.00.20404 for
Microsoft (R) .NET Framework version 3.5
Copyright (C) Microsoft Corporation. All rights reserved.
```

First.exe

```
This isn't at all like Java!
```

Well, maybe that message isn't quite true! This program has some fairly fundamental similarities to Java, although there are one or two points (such as the capitalized Main() function) to catch the unwary
Java or C++ developer. Let's look more closely at what's going on in the code.

❖ Using Comments

The next topic — adding comments to your code — looks very simple on the surface but can be complex.

Internal Comments within the Source Files

C# uses the traditional C-type single-line (// ...) and multiline (/* ... */) comments:

// This is a single-line comment /* This
comment
    spans multiple lines. */

Everything in a single-line comment, from the // to the end of the line, will be ignored by the compiler, and everything from an opening /* to the next */ in a multiline comment combination will be ignored. Obviously, you can't include the combination */ in any multiline comments, because this will be treated as the end of the comment.

It is actually possible to put multiline comments within a line of code:

Console.WriteLine(/* Here's a comment! */ "This will compile.");

Use inline comments with care because they can make code hard to read. However, they can be useful when debugging if, say, you temporarily want to try running the code with a different value somewhere:

DoSomething(Width, /*Height*/ 100);

Comment characters included in string literals are, of course, treated like normal characters:

string s = "/* This is just a normal string .*/";

XML Documentation

In addition to the C-type comments, illustrated in the preceding section, C# has a very neat feature that we want to highlight: the ability to produce documentation in XML format automatically from special comments. These comments are single-line comments but begin with three slashes (///) instead of the usual two. Within these comments, you can place XML tags containing documentation of the types and type members in your code.

The tags in the following table are recognized by the compiler.

Tag	Description
<c>	Marks up text within a line as code, for example <c>int i = 10;</c>.
<code>	Marks multiple lines as code.
<example>	Marks up a code example.
<exception>	Documents an exception class. (Syntax is verified by the compiler.)
<include>	Includes comments from another documentation file. (Syntax is verified by the compiler.)
<list>	Inserts a list into the documentation.
<param>	Marks up a method parameter. (Syntax is verified by the compiler.)
<paramref>	Indicates that a word is a method parameter. (Syntax is verified by the compiler.)
<permission>	Documents access to a member. (Syntax is verified by the compiler.)
<remarks>	Adds a description for a member.
<returns>	Documents the return value for a method.
<see>	Provides a cross-reference to another parameter. (Syntax is verified by the compiler.)
<seealso>	Provides a "see also" section in a description. (Syntax is verified by the compiler.)
<summary>	Provides a short summary of a type or member.
<value>	Describes a property.

To see how this works, add some XML comments to the MathLibrary.cs file from the "More on Compiling C# Files" section, and call it Math.cs. You will add a <summary> element for the class and for its Add() method, and also a <returns> element and two <param> elements for the Add() method:

```
// Math.cs
namespace Wrox.ProCSharp.Basics
{

    ///<summary>
    ///    Wrox.ProCSharp.Basics.Math class.
    ///    Provides a method to add two integers.
    ///</summary>
    public class Math
    {
        ///<summary>
        ///    The Add method allows us to add two integers.
        ///</summary>
        ///<returns>Result of the addition (int)</returns>
        ///<param name="x">First number to add</param>
        ///<param name="y">Second number to
        add</param> public int Add(int x, int y)
        {
```

```
    return x + y;
  }
 }
}
```

The C# compiler can extract the XML elements from the special comments and use them to generate an XML file. To get the compiler to generate the XML documentation for an assembly, you specify the /doc option when you compile, together with the name of the file you want to be created:

    csc /t:library /doc:Math.xml Math.cs

The compiler will throw an error if the XML comments do not result in a well-formed XML document.

This will generate an XML file named Math.xml, which looks like this:

```
<?xml version="1.0"?>
<doc>
  <assembly>
    <name>Math</name>
  </assembly>
  <members>
    <member
      name="T:Wrox.ProCSharp.Basics.Math">
      <summary>
        Wrox.ProCSharp.Basics.Math class. Provides
        a method to add two integers.
      </summary>
    </member>
    <member name=
        "M:Wrox.ProCSharp.Basics.Math.Add(System.Int32,System.Int32)">
      <summary>
        The Add method allows us to add two integers.
      </summary>
      <returns>Result of the addition (int)</returns>
      <param name="x">First number to add</param>
      <param name="y">Second number to add</param>
    </member>
  </members>
</doc>
```

Notice how the compiler has actually done some work for you; it has created an <assembly> element and also added a <member> element for each type or member of a type in the file. Each <member> element has a name attribute with the full name of the member as its value, prefixed by a letter that indicates whether this is a type (T:), field (F:), or member (M:).

❖ Using Comments

Exception handling is an in built mechanism in .NET framework to detect and handle run time errors. The .NET framework contains lots of standard exceptions. The exceptions are anomalies that occur during the execution of a program. They can be because of user, logic or system errors. If a user (programmer) do not provide a mechanism to handle these anomalies, the .NET run time environment provide a default mechanism, which terminates the program execution.

C# provides three keywords try, catch and finally to do exception handling. The try encloses the statements that might throw an exception whereas catch handles an exception if one exists. The finally can be used for doing any clean up process.

The general form try-catch-finally in C# is shown below

```
try
{
    // Statement which can cause an exception.
}
catch(Type x)
{
    // Statements for handling the exception
}
finally
{
    //Any cleanup code
}
```

If any exception occurs inside the try block, the control transfers to the appropriate catch block and later to the finally block.

But in C#, both catch and finally blocks are optional. The try block can exist either with one or more catch blocks or a finally block or with both catch and finally blocks.

If there is no exception occurred inside the try block, the control directly transfers to finally block. We can say that the statements inside the finally block is executed always. Note that it is an error to transfer control out of a finally block by using break, continue, return or goto.

In C#, exceptions are nothing but objects of the type Exception. The Exception is the ultimate base class for any exceptions in C#. The C# itself provides couple of standard exceptions. Or even the user can create their own exception classes, provided that this should inherit from either Exception class or one of the standard derived classes of Exception class like DivideByZeroExcpetion ot ArgumentException etc.

Uncaught Exceptions

The following program will compile but will show an error during execution. The division by zero is a runtime anomaly and program terminates with an error message. Any uncaught exceptions in the current context propagate to a higher context and looks for an appropriate catch block to handle it. If it can't find any suitable catch blocks, the default mechanism of the .NET runtime will terminate the execution of the entire program.

```
//C#: Exception Handling
usingSystem;
class MyClient
{
    public static void Main()
    {
        int x = 0;
        int div = 100/x;
        Console.WriteLine(div);
    }
}
```

The modified form of the above program with exception handling mechanism is as follows. Here we are using the object of the standard exception class DivideByZeroException to handle the exception caused by division by zero.

```
//C#: Exception Handling
using System;
class MyClient
{
    public static void Main()
    {
        int x = 0;
        int div = 0;
        try
        {
            div = 100/x;
            Console.WriteLine("This line in not executed");
        }
        catch(DivideByZeroException de)
        {
            Console.WriteLine("Exception occured");
        }
        Console.WriteLine("Result is {0}",div);
    }
}
```

In the above case the program do not terminate unexpectedly. Instead the program control passes from the point where exception occurred inside the try block to the catch blocks. If it finds any suitable catch block, executes the statements inside that catch and continues with the normal execution of the program statements.
If a finally block is present, the code inside the finally block will get also be executed.

```
//C#: Exception Handling
using System;
class MyClient
{
    public static void Main()
    {
        int x = 0;
        int div = 0;
        try
        {
            div = 100/x;
            Console.WriteLine("Not executed line");
        }
```

```
catch(DivideByZeroException de)
{
        Console.WriteLine("Exception occured");
}
finally
{
        Console.WriteLine("Finally Block");
}
Console.WriteLine("Result is {0}",div);
    }
}
```

Remember that in C#, the catch block is optional. The following program is perfectly legal in C#.

```
//C#: Exception Handling
using System;
class MyClient
{
    public static void Main()
    {
        int x = 0;
        int div = 0;
        try
        {
                div = 100/x;
                Console.WriteLine("Not executed line");
        }
        finally
        {
                Console.WriteLine("Finally Block");
        }
        Console.WriteLine("Result is {0}",div);
    }
}
```

But in this case, since there is no exception handling catch block, the execution will get terminated. But before the termination of the program statements inside the finally block will get executed. In C#, a try block must be followed by either a catch or finally block.

Multiple Catch Blocks

A try block can throw multiple exceptions, which can handle by using multiple catch blocks. Remember that more specialized catch block should come before a generalized one. Otherwise the compiler will show a compilation error.

```
//C#: Exception Handling: Multiple catch
using System;
class MyClient
{
    public static void Main()
    {
        int x = 0;
        int div = 0;
```

```
        try
        {
                div = 100/x;
                Console.WriteLine("Not executed line");
        }
        catch(DivideByZeroException de)
        {
                Console.WriteLine("DivideByZeroException" );
        }
        catch(Exception ee)
        {
                Console.WriteLine("Exception" );
        }
        finally
        {
                Console.WriteLine("Finally Block");
        }
        Console.WriteLine("Result is {0}",div);
    }
}
```

Catching all Exceptions

By providing a catch block without a brackets or arguments, we can catch all exceptions occurred inside a try block. Even we can use a catch block with an Exception type parameter to catch all exceptions happened inside the try block since in C#, all exceptions are directly or indirectly inherited from the Exception class.

```
//C#: Exception Handling: Handling all exceptions
using System;
class MyClient
{
    public static void Main()
    {
            int x = 0;
            int div = 0;
            try
            {
                    div = 100/x;
                    Console.WriteLine("Not executed line");
            }
            Catch
            {
                    Console.WriteLine("oException" );
            }
            Console.WriteLine("Result is {0}",div);
    }
}
```

The following program handles all exception with Exception object.

```
//C#: Exception Handling: Handling all exceptions
using System;
class MyClient
{
    public static void Main()
```

```
{
    int x = 0;
    int div = 0;
    try
    {
        div = 100/x;
        Console.WriteLine("Not executed line");
    }
    catch(Exception e)
    {
        Console.WriteLine("oException" );
    }
    Console.WriteLine("Result is {0}",div);
}
}
```

Throwing an Exception

In C#, it is possible to throw an exception programmatically. The 'throw' keyword is used for this purpose. The general form of throwing an exception is as follows.

throw exception_obj;

For example the following statement throw an ArgumentException explicitly.

throw new ArgumentException("Exception");

```
//C#: Exception Handling:
using System;
class MyClient
{
    public static void Main()
    {
        try
        {
            throw new DivideByZeroException("Invalid Division");
        }
        catch(DivideByZeroException e)
        {
            Console.WriteLine("Exception" );
        }
        Console.WriteLine("LAST STATEMENT");
    }
}
```

Re-throwing an Exception

The exceptions, which we caught inside a catch block, can re-throw to a higher context by using the keyword throw inside the catch block. The following program shows how to do this.

```
//C#: Exception Handling: Handling all exceptions
using System;
class MyClass
{
    public void Method()
```

```
{
        try
        {
                int x = 0;
                int sum = 100/x;
        }
        catch(DivideByZeroException e)
        {
                throw;
        }
}
}
class MyClient
{
    public static void Main()
    {
        MyClass mc = new MyClass();
        try
        {
                mc.Method();
        }
        catch(Exception e)
        {
                Console.WriteLine("Exception caught here" );


        Console.WriteLine("LAST STATEMENT");
    }
}
```

Standard Exceptions

There are two types of exceptions: exceptions generated by an executing program and exceptions generated by the common language runtime. System.Exception is the base class for all exceptions in C#. Several exception classes inherit from this class including ApplicationException and SystemException. These two classes form the basis for most other runtime exceptions. Other exceptions that derive directly from System.Exception include IOException, WebException etc.

The common language runtime throws SystemException. The ApplicationException is thrown by a user program rather than the runtime. The SystemException includes the ExecutionEngineException, StaclOverFlowException etc. It is not recommended that we catch SystemExceptions nor is it good programming practice to throw SystemExceptions in our applications.

- System.OutOfMemoryException
- System.NullReferenceException
- Syste.InvalidCastException
- Syste.ArrayTypeMismatchException
- System.IndexOutOfRangeException
- System.ArithmeticException
- System.DevideByZeroException
- System.OverFlowException

User-defined Exceptions

In C#, it is possible to create our own exception class. But Exception must be the ultimate base class for all exceptions in C#. So the user-defined exception classes must inherit from either Exception class or one of its standard derived classes.

```csharp
//C#: Exception Handling: User defined exceptions
using System;
class MyException : Exception
{
    public MyException(string str)
    {
        Console.WriteLine("User defined exception");
    }
}
class MyClient
{
    public static void Main()
    {
        Try
        {
            throw new MyException("RAJESH");
        }
        catch(Exception e)
        {
            Console.WriteLine("Exception caught here" + e.ToString());
        }
        Console.WriteLine("LAST STATEMENT");
    }
}
```

Chapter 2: C# - Basics

❖ Introduction to C# .NET Language

C# is a simple, modern, object oriented, and type-safe programming language derived from C and C++. It will immediately be familiar to C and C++ programmers. C# aims to combine the high productivity of Visual Basic and the raw power of C++.

In addition to C#, Visual Studio supports Visual Basic, Visual C++, and the scripting languages VBScript and JScript. All of these languages provide access to the Microsoft .NET platform, which includes a common execution engine and a rich class library. The Microsoft .NET platform defines a "Common Language Specification" (CLS), a sort of lingua franca that ensures seamless interoperability between CLS-compliant languages and class libraries. For C# developers, this means that even though C# is a new language, it has complete access to the same rich class libraries that are used by seasoned tools such as Visual Basic and Visual C++. C# itself does not include a class library.

The canonical "hello, world" program can be written as follows:

```
using System;
class Hello
{
        static void Main() {
            Console.WriteLine("hello, world");
        }
}
```

The source code for a C# program is typically stored in one or more text files with a file extension of .cs, as in hello.cs. Using the command-line compiler provided with Visual Studio, such a program can be compiled with the command line directive

```
csc hello.cs
```

Which produces an executable program named hello.exe. The output of the program is:

hello, world

Close examination of this program is illuminating:

The using System; directive references a namespace called System that is provided by the Microsoft .NET Framework class library. This namespace contains the Console class referred to in the Main method. Namespaces provide a hierarchical means of organizing the elements of a class library or program. A "using" directive enables unqualified use of the types that are members of the namespace. The "hello, world" program uses Console.WriteLine as a shorthand for System.Console.WriteLine.

The Main method is a member of the class Hello. It has the static modifier, and so it is a method on the class Hello rather than on instances of this class.

The main entry point for a program—the method that is called to begin execution—is always a static method named Main.

The "hello, world" output is produced through the use of a class library. The language does not itself provide a class library. Instead, it uses a common class library that is also used by languages such as Visual Basic and Visual C++.

❖ Variables

You declare variables in C# using the following syntax:
    datatype identifier;
For example:
    int i;
This statement declares an int named i . The compiler won ' t actually let you use this variable in anexpression until you have initialized it with a value.
Once it has been declared, you can assign a value to the variable using the assignment operator, =:
    i = 10;
You can also declare the variable and initialize its value at the same time:
    int i = 10;
This syntax is identical to C++ and Java syntax but very different from Visual Basic syntax for declaring variables. If you are coming from Visual Basic 6, you should also be aware that C# doesn ' t distinguish between objects and simple types, so there is no need for anything like the Set keyword, even if you want your variable to refer to an object. The C# syntax for declaring variables is the same no matter what the data type of the variable.

If you declare and initialize more than one variable in a single statement, all of the variables will be of the same data type:
    int x = 10, y =20; // x and y are both ints
To declare variables of different types, you need to use separate statements. You cannot assign different data types within a multiple variable declaration:
    int x = 10;
    bool y = true; // Creates a variable that stores true or false
    int x = 10, bool y = true; // This won't compile!
Notice the // and the text after it in the preceding examples. These are comments. The // character sequence tells the compiler to ignore the text that follows on this line because it is for a human to better understand the program and not part of the program itself.

➢ Initialization of Variables

Variable initialization demonstrates an example of C# ' s emphasis on safety. Briefly, the C# compiler requires that any variable be initialized with some starting value before you refer to that variable in an operation. Most modern compilers will flag violations of this as a warning, but the ever - vigilant C# compiler treats such violations as errors. This prevents you from unintentionally retrieving junk values from memory that is left over from other programs.

C# has two methods for ensuring that variables are initialized before use:

- ✓ Variables that are fields in a class or struct, if not initialized explicitly, are by default zeroed out when they are created (classes and structs are discussed later).
- ✓ Variables that are local to a method must be explicitly initialized in your code prior to any statements in which their values are used. In this case, the initialization doesn ' t have to happen when the variable is declared, but the compiler will check all

possible paths through the method and will flag an error if it detects any possibility of the value of a local variable being used before it is initialized.
C# ' s approach contrasts with C++ ' s approach, in which the compiler leaves it up to the programmer to make sure that variables are initialized before use, and with Visual Basic ' s approach, in which all variables are zeroed out automatically.

For example, you can ' t do the following in C#:

```
public static int Main()
{
        int d;
        Console.WriteLine(d); // Can't do this! Need to initialize d before use
        return 0;
}
```

Notice that this code snippet demonstrates defining Main() so that it returns an int instead of void .

When you attempt to compile these lines, you will receive this error message:
    Use of unassigned local variable 'd'
Consider the following statement:
    Something objSomething;

In C++, this line would create an instance of the Something class on the stack. In C#, this same line of code would create only a reference for a Something object, but this reference would not yet actually refer to any object. Any attempt to call a method or property against this variable would result in an error.

Instantiating a reference object in C# requires use of the new keyword. You create a reference as shown in the previous example and then point the reference at an object allocated on the heap using the new keyword:
    objSomething = new Something(); // This creates a Something on the heap

➢ Variable Scope

The scope of a variable is the region of code from which the variable can be accessed. In general, the scope is determined by the following rules:

- ✓ A *field* (also known as a member variable) of a class is in scope for as long as its containing class is in scope (this is the same as for C++, Java, and VB).
- ✓ A *local variable* is in scope until a closing brace indicates the end of the block statement or method in which it was declared.
- ✓ A local variable that is declared in a for , while , or similar statement is in scope in the body of that loop. (C++ developers will recognize that this is the same behavior as the ANSI standard for C++. Early versions of the Microsoft C++ compiler did not comply with this standard but scoped such variables to remain in scope after the loop terminated.)

❖ Contants

As the name implies, a constant is a variable whose value cannot be changed throughout its lifetime.

Prefixing a variable with the const keyword when it is declared and initialized designates that variable

as a constant:

const int a = 100; // This value cannot be changed.

Constants will be familiar to Visual Basic and C++ developers. C++ developers should, however, note that C# does not permit all the subtleties of C++ constants. In C++, not only could variables be declared as constant, but depending on the declaration, you could have constant pointers, variable pointers to constants, constant methods (that don't change the contents of the containing object), constant parameters to methods, and so on. These subtleties have been discarded in C#, and all you can do is declare local variables and fields to be constant.

Constants have the following characteristics:

They must be initialized when they are declared, and once a value has been assigned, it can never be overwritten.

The value of a constant must be computable at compile time. Therefore, you can't initialize a constant with a value taken from a variable. If you need to do this, you will need to use a read - only field.

Constants are always implicitly static. However, notice that you don't have to (and, in fact, are not permitted to) include the static modifier in the constant declaration.

At least three advantages exist to using constants in your programs:

Constants make your programs easier to read by replacing magic numbers and strings with readable names whose values are easy to understand.

Constants make your programs easier to modify. For example, assume that you have a SalesTax constant in one of your C# programs, and that constant is assigned a value of 6 percent. If the sales tax rate changes at a later point in time, you can modify the behavior of all tax calculations simply by assigning a new value to the constant; you don't have to hunt throughout your code for the value .06 and change each one, hoping that you will find all of them.

Constants help to prevent mistakes in your programs. If you attempt to assign another value to a constant somewhere in your program other than at the point where the constant is declared, the compiler will flag the error.

❖ Strings

A string is basically a sequence of characters. Each character is a Unicode character in the range U+0000 to U+FFFF.

System.String is a class specifically designed to store a string and allow a large number of operations on the string. In addition, due to the importance of this data type, C# has its own keyword and associated syntax to make it particularly easy to manipulate strings using this class.

You can concatenate strings using operator overloads:

string message1 = "Hello"; // returns "Hello"

message1 += ", There"; // returns "Hello, There"

string message2 = message1 + "!"; // returns "Hello, There!"

C# also allows extraction of a particular character using an indexer - like syntax:

char char4 = message[4]; // returns 'a'. Note the char is zero-indexed

String class Members

String class provides two properties - Chars and Length. The Chars property returns the character at a specified position in a string and the Length property returns the number of characters in a string.

String class provides two types of methods - static and instance. Static methods can only be used by String class, not by an instance of the String class. The instance methods are used by instances of the String class.

Method	Description
Compare	This method compares two specified String objects.
CompareOrdinal	This method compares two **String** objects, without considering the local national language or culture.
Concat	This method concatenates one or more **Strings**.
Copy	This method creates a new instance of String with the same value as a specified **String**.
Format	This method replaces each format specification in a specified **String** with the textual equivalent of a corresponding object's value.
Intern	This method returns the system's reference to the specified **String**.
IsInterned	This method returns a reference to a specified **String**.
Join	This method concatenates a specified separator **String** between each element of a specified **String** array, yielding a single concatenated string.

Table 1: The String class static methods

Method	Description
Clone	This method returns a reference to this instance of **String**.
CompareTo	This method compares a string with another.
CopyTo	This method copies a specified number of characters from a specified position in this instance to a specified position in an array of characters.
EndsWith	This method determines whether the end of this instance matches a string.
IndexOf	This method reports the index of the first occurrence of a string, or one or more characters, within this instance.
IndexOfAny	This method reports the index of the first occurrence in this instance of any character in a specified array of Unicode characters.
Insert	This method inserts a string at a specified index position.
LastIndexOf	This method returns the index position of the last occurrence of a specified character.
LastIndexOfAny	This method reports the index position of the last occurrence of one on more characters in a string.
PadLeft	This method right-aligns the characters in a string, padding on the left with spaces or a specified character for a specified total length.
PadRight	This method left-aligns the characters in a string, padding on the right with spaces or a specified character, for a specified total length.
Remove	This method deletes a specified number of characters from a string beginning at a specified position.
Replace	This method replaces all occurrences of a specified character or string with another specified character or string.
Split	This method identifies the substrings in this instance that are delimited by one or more characters specified in an array, then places the substrings into a string array.
StartsWith	This method determines whether the beginning of a string matches with a string.
Substring	This method returns a substring from a string.
ToCharArray	This method copies the characters in this instance to a Unicode character array.
ToLower	This method returns a copy of a string in lowercase.
ToUpper	This method returns a copy of a string in uppercase.
Trim	This method deletes all occurrences of a set of specified characters from the beginning and end of a string.
TrimEnd	This method deletes all occurrences of a set of characters specified in a character array from the end of a string.

Table 2: The String class instance methods

Comparing Strings

The Compare method compares two strings and returns an integer value. The return value of Compare method can be less than zero, greater than zero or equals to zero.

Value	Meaning
Less than zero	When first string is less than second.
Zero	When both strings are equal.
Greater than zero	When first string is greater than zero.

The following code compares two strings and return results on the System console.

```
// Comparing two strings
//===================================
string str1 = "ppp";
string str2 = "ccc";
int res = String.Compare(str1, str2);
Console.WriteLine("First result:" +res.ToString());
str2 = "ttt"; res = String.Compare(str1, str2);
Console.WriteLine("Second result:" +res.ToString());
str1 = "ttt"; res = String.Compare(str1, str2);
Console.WriteLine("Third result:" +res.ToString());
//===================================
```

The CompareTo method is an instance method. It compares a value (either a string or on object) with a string instance. Return values of this method are same as the Compare method. The following source code compares two strings.

```
// CompareTo Method
string str = "kkk";
Console.WriteLine( str.CompareTo(str1) );
```

Copy and Concatenating Strings

The Concat method adds strings (or objects) and returns a new string. Using Concat method, you can add two strings, two objects and one string and one object or more combinations of these two.

The following source code concatenate two strings.

```
string str1 = "ppp";
string str2 = "ccc";
string strRes = String.Concat(str1, str2);
Console.WriteLine(strRes);
```

The following source code concatenates one string and one object.

```
object obj = (object)12;
strRes = String.Concat(str1, obj);
Console.WriteLine(strRes);
```

The Copy method copies contents of a string to another. The Copy method takes a string as input and returns another string with the same contents as the input string. For example, the following code copies str1 to strRes.

```
string str1 = "ppp";
string str2 = "ccc";
string strRes = String.Copy(str1);
Console.WriteLine("Copy result :" + strRes);
```

The CopyTo method copies a specified number of characters from a specified position in this instance to a specified position in an array of characters. For example, the following example copies contents of str1 to an array

C# Programming Made Easy

of characters. You can also specify the starting character of a string and number of characters you want to copy to the array.

```
string str1 = "ppp";
char[] chrs = new Char[2];
str1.CopyTo(0, chrs, 0, 2);
```

The Clone method returns a new copy of a string in form of object. The following code creates a clone of str1.

```
string str1 = "ppp";
object objClone = str1.Clone();
Console.WriteLine("Clone :"+objClone.ToString());
```

The Join method is useful when you need to insert a separator (String) between each element of a string array, yielding a single concatenated string. For example, the following sample inserts a comma and space (", ") between each element of an array of strings.

```
string str1 = "ppp";
string str2 = "ccc";
string str3 = "kkk";
string[] allStr = new String[]{str1, str2, str3};
string strRes = String.Join(", ", allStr);
Console.WriteLine("Join Results: "+ strRes);
```

Adding, Removing and Replacing Strings

The Insert method inserts a specified string at a specified index position in an instance. For example, the following source code inserts "bbb" after second character in str1 and the result string is "pbbbpp".

```
string str1 = "ppp";
string strRes = str1.Insert(2, "bbb");
Console.WriteLine(strRes.ToString());
```

The Remove method deletes a specified number of characters from a specified position in a string. This method returns result as a string. For example, the following code removes three characters from index 3.

```
string s = "123abc000";
Console.WriteLine(s.Remove(3, 3));
```

The Replace method replaces all occurrences of a specified character in a string. For example, the following source code replaces all p character instances of str1 with character I and returns string "III".

```
string str1 = "ppp";
string repStr = str1.Replace('p', 'I');
Console.WriteLine("Replaced string:"+ repStr.ToString() );
```

The Split method separates strings by a specified set of characters and places these strings into an array of strings. For example, the following source code splits strArray based on ',' and stores all separated strings in an array.

```
string str1 = "ppp";
string str2 = "ccc";
string str3 = "kkk";
string strAll3 = str1 + ", " +str2+", "+str3 ;
string[] strArray = strAll3.Split(',');
foreach (string itm in strArray)
{
Console.WriteLine(itm.ToString() );
}
```

Uppercase and Lowercase

The ToUpper and ToLower methods convert a string in uppercase and lowercase respectively. These methods are easy to use. The following code shows how to use ToUppler and ToLower methods.

```
string aStr = "adgas";
string bStr = "ABNMDWER";
string strRes = aStr.ToUpper();
Console.WriteLine("Uppercase:"+ strRes.ToString());
strRes = bStr.ToLower();
Console.WriteLine("Lowercase:"+ strRes.ToString());
```

Initializing a String

Actually String class provides eight-overloaded form of constructor methods. These constructors are described in Table 1.

Constructor	Description
unsafe public String(char*);	Creates a new instance from a specified pointer to an array of Unicode characters.
public String(char[]);	Creates a new instance from an array of Unicode characters.
unsafe public String(sbyte*);	Creates a new instance from a pointer to an array of 8-bit signed integers.
public String(char, int);	Creates a new instance from a Unicode character repeated a specified number of times.
unsafe public String(char*, int, int);	Creates a new instance from an array of Unicode character, a starting character position within that array and a length.
public String(char[], int, int);	Create a new instance from an array of Unicode characters, a starting character position within the array and a length.
unsafe public String(sbyte*, int, int);	Create a new instance from an array of 8-bit signed integer, a starting character position within the array and a length.
unsafe public String(sbyte*, int, int, Encoding);	Create a new instance from a pointer of array of 8-bit signed integer, a starting character position within the array and a length and an Encoding Object.

Table 1: The String class constructors

C# Programming Made Easy

Formatting Strings

You can use the **Format** method to create formatted strings and concatenate multiple strings representing multiple objects. The Format method automatically converts any passed object into a string.

For example, the following code uses integer, floating number and string values and format them into a string using the Format method.

Listing 1: Using Format method to format a string

```
int val = 7;
string name = "Mr. John";
float num = 45.06f;
string str = String.Format ("Days Left : {0}. Current DataTime: {1:u}. \n String: {2}, Float: {3}" , val, DateTime.Now,
name, num);
Console.WriteLine(str);
```

The output of Listing 1 is shown Figure 1.

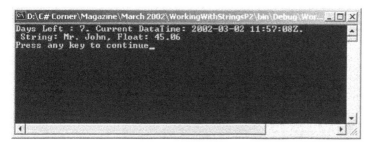

Figure 1.

Trimming and Removing Characters from Strings

The String class provides Trim, TrimStart and TrimEnd methods to trim strings. The Trim method removes white spaces from the beginning and end of a string. The TrimEnd method removes characters specified in an array of characters from the end of a string and TrimStart method removes characters specified in an array of characters from the beginning of a string.

You can also use the Remove method to remove characters from a string. The Listing 2 code shows how to use these methods.

```
String str = " C# ";
Console.WriteLine("Hello{0}World!", str);
string trStr = str.Trim();
Console.WriteLine("Hello{0}World!", trStr );
str = "Hello World!";
char[] chArr = {'e', 'H','l','o',' ' };
trStr = str.TrimStart(chArr);
Console.WriteLine(trStr);
str = "Hello World!";
char[] chArr1 = {'e', 'H','l','o',' ' };
trStr = str.TrimEnd(chArr1);
Console.WriteLine(trStr);
```

```
string MyString = "Hello Delta World!";
Console.WriteLine(MyString.Remove(5,10));
```

Padding Strings

The PadLeft and PadRight methods can be used to pad strings. The PadLeft method right-aligns and pads a string so that its rightmost character is the specified distance from the beginning of the string. The PadRight method left-aligns and pads a string so that its rightmost character is a specified distance from the end of the string. These methods return new String objects that can either be padded with empty spaces or with custom characters. Listign 3 shows how to use these methods.

Listing 3: Using padding methods

```
string str1 = "My String";
Console.WriteLine(str1.PadLeft(20, '-'));
string str2 = "My String";
Console.WriteLine(str2.PadRight(20, '-'));
```

The output of Listing 3 is shown in Figure 2.

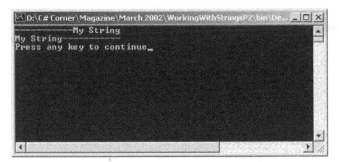

Figure 2.

The StringBuilder Class

The StringBuilder class represents a mutable string of characters. It's called mutable because it can be modified once it has been created by using Append, Insert, Remove, and Replace methods.

The StringBuilder class is defined in the System.Text namespace. Before you use the StringBuilder class make sure you add the following line in your application:

```
using System.Text;
```

C# Programming Made Easy

Table 2 describes the StringBuilder class properties

Property	Description
Capacity	Represents the maximum number of characters that can be contained in the memory allocated by the current instance.
Chars	Represents the character at the specified position.
Length	Represents the number of characters.
MaxCapacity	Returns the maximum capacity.

Table 2: The StringBuilder class properties

Table 3 describes the StringBuilder class methods

Method	Description
Append	Appends a string at the end of this string.
AppendFormat	Appends a formatted string.
EnsureCapaciry	Ensures that the capacity of string is as specified value.
Inserts	Inserts string at the specified position.
Remove	Removes a range of characters from the string.
Replace	Replaces all occurrences of a character from the string.

Table 3. The StringBuilder class methods.

Using StringBuilder properties and methods is pretty simple. Listing 4 uses StringBuilder class to append, insert, remove and replace characters of a string.

Listing 4. Using StringBuilder class to append, add, replace and remove characters

```
StringBuilder builder = new StringBuilder("Hello C# World!", 20);
StringBuilder builder = new StringBuilder("Hello C# World!", 20);
int cap = builder.EnsureCapacity(55);
builder.Append(". This is a class test.");
Console.WriteLine(builder);
builder.Insert(26," String Builder");
Console.WriteLine(builder);
builder.Remove(5, 9);
Console.WriteLine(builder);
builder.Replace('!', '?');
Console.WriteLine(builder);
Console.WriteLine("Length of string is:" + builder.Length.ToString() );
Console.WriteLine("Capacity of string is:" + builder.Capacity.ToString() );
```

The output of Listing 4 is shown in Figure 3.

```
D:\C# Corner\Magazine\March 2002\WorkingWithStringsP2\bin\Debug\Wor...
Hello C# World!. This is a class test.
Hello C# World!. This is a String Builder class test.
Hello!. This is a String Builder class test.
Hello?. This is a String Builder class test.
Length of string is:44
Capacity of string is:56
Press any key to continue_
```

Figure 3.

❖ Data Types

A programming language wouldn't be able to do much if it didn't have data to work with. C# supports two data types: value types and reference types. *Value types* are the typical primitive types available in most programming languages and are allocated on the stack. *Reference types* are typically class instances and are allocated on the heap. Both are discussed in further detail in the following sections

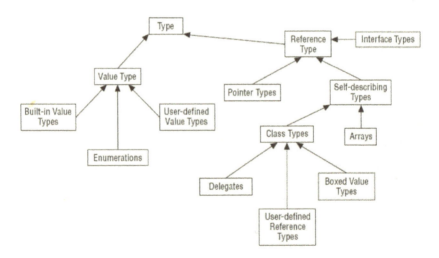

➤ Value Types

Value types encompass the data types you would traditionally encounter in nonobject-oriented programming languages.This includes numeric, strings, bytes, and Booleans.Value types in C# are implemented in the form of Structures and Enums.Value types are allocated on the stack and therefore have little overhead associated with them.

o **Predefined Value Types**

▪ **Integer Types**
int is short for integer, a data type for storing numbers without decimals. When working with numbers, int is the most commonly used data type. Integers have several data types within C#, depending on the size of the number they are supposed to store.

▪ **Floating - Point Types**
The float data type is for smaller floating - point values, for which less precision is required. The double data type is bulkier than the float data type but offers twice the precision (15 digits). If you hard - code a non - integer number (such as 12.3) in your code, the compiler will normally assume that you want the number interpreted as a double . If you want to specify that the value is a float , you append the character F (or f) to it:

    float f = 12.3F;

▪ **Decimal Types**
The decimal type represents higher - precision floating - point numbers.
One of the great things about the CTS and C# is the provision of a dedicated decimal type for financial calculations. How you use the 28 digits that the decimal type provides is up to you. In other words, you can track smaller dollar amounts with greater accuracy for cents or larger dollar amounts with more rounding in the fractional area. Bear in mind, however, that decimal is not implemented under the hood as a primitive type, so using decimal will have a performance effect on your calculations.
To specify that your number is a decimal type rather than a double , float , or an integer, you can append the M (or m) character to the value, as shown in the following example:
decimal d = 12.30M;

▪ **Boolean Types**
The C# bool type is used to contain Boolean values of either true or false
You cannot implicitly convert bool values to and from integer values. If a variable (or a function return type) is declared as a bool , you can only use values of true and false . You will get an error if you try to use zero for false and a non - zero value for true , as is possible to do in C++.

▪ **Character Types**
For storing the value of a single character, C# supports the char data type.
Although this data type has a superficial resemblance to the char type provided by C and C++, there is a significant difference. A C++ char represents an 8 - bit character, whereas a C# char contains 16 bits. This is part of the reason that implicit conversions between the char type and the 8 - bit byte type are not permitted. Although 8 bits may be enough to encode every character in the English language and the digits 0 – 9, they aren ' t enough to encode every character in more expansive symbol systems (such as Chinese). In a gesture toward universality, the computer industry is moving away from the 8 - bit character set and toward the 16 - bit Unicode scheme, of which the ASCII encoding is a subset. Literals of type char are signified by being enclosed in single

quotation marks, for example ' A ' . If you try to enclose a character in double quotation marks, the compiler will treat this as a string and throw an error.

Data Type	CTS Type	Description	Range
byte	System.Byte	8 - bit unsigned integer	0:255 (0:2^8 - 1)
sbyte	System.SByte	8 - bit signed integer	- 128:127 (- 2^7 :2^7 - 1)
short	System.Int16	16 - bit signed integer	- 32,768:32,767 (- 2^15 :2^15 - 1)
ushort	System.UInt16	16 - bit unsigned integer	0:65,535 (0:2^16 - 1)
int	System.Int32	32 - bit signed integer	- 2^31 :2^31 – 1
uint	System.UInt32	32 - bit unsigned integer	0:2^32 - 1
long	System.Int64	64 - bit signed integer	- 2^63 :2^63 - 1
ulong	System.UInt64	64 - bit unsigned integer	0:2^64 - 1
float	System.Single	32-bit single-precision floating point	±1.5 × 10^-45 to ±3.4 × 10^38(7 Significant Figures)
double	System.Double	64-bit double-precision floating point	±5.0 × 10^-324 to ±1.7 × 10^308(15/16 Significant Figures)
decimal	System.Decimal	128 - bit high – precision decimal notation	± 1.0 × 10^-28 to ± 7.9 × 10^28(28 Significant Figures)
bool	System.Boolean	Represents true or false	true false
string	System.String	Unicode character string	
char	System.Char	System.Char Represents a single 16 - bit (Unicode) character	
object	System.Object	The root type. All other types in the CTS are erived (including value types) rom object .	

> **Reference Types**

Instances of classes are reference types. Reference types are allocated on the heap. In C#, all classes are derived from the .NET Framework class *Object* within the *System* namespace. C# does not support pointers, but classes, being reference data types, act like pointers. If you copy a pointer to another pointer, they both still reference the same object.You can modify the contents of the original object from either pointer. In C#, if you instantiate a class object and then make a copy of it, changes made to either instance of the class change the original object. If you pass an instance of a class to a class method, changes made to the object passed in will persist upon returning from the method call. As we mentioned previously, reference types are allocated on the heap.The *new* keyword is used to allocate a new instance of a reference type (class).You don't need to free an instance of a class in C#, however.The CLR does garbage collection on object instances that are no longer referenced.

- The *object* Types

Many programming languages and class hierarchies provide a root type, from which all other objects in the hierarchy are derived. C# and .NET are no exception. In C#, the object type is the ultimate parent type from which all other intrinsic and user - defined types are derived. This is a key feature of C# that distinguishes it from both Visual Basic 6.0 and C++, although its behavior here is very similar to Java. All types implicitly derive ultimately from the System.Object class. This means that you can use the object type for two purposes:

- ✓ You can use an object reference to bind to an object of any particular subtype. object references are also useful in reflection, when code must manipulate objects whose specific types are unknown. This is similar to the role played by a void pointer in C++ or by a Variant data type in VB.
- ✓ The object type implements a number of basic, general - purpose methods, which include Equals() , GetHashCode() , GetType() , and ToString() . Responsible user - defined classes may need to provide replacement implementations of some of these methods using an object - oriented technique known as *overriding*. If you don ' t provide your own implementations for these methods in your classes, the compiler will pick up the implementations in object , which may or may not be correct or sensible in the context of your classes.

- The *string* Types

A C or C++ string is nothing more than an array of characters, so the client programmer has to do a lot of work just to copy one string to another or to concatenate two strings. In fact, for a generation of C++ programmers, implementing a string class that raps up the messy details of these operations was a rite of passage requiring many hours of teeth gnashing and head scratching. Visual Basic programmers have a somewhat easier life, with a string type, and Java people have it even better, with a String class that is in many ways very similar to a C# string. C# recognizes the string keyword, which under the hood is translated to the .NET class, System.String . With it, operations like string concatenation and string copying are a snap:

```
string str1 = "Hello ";
string str2 = "World";
string str3 = str1 + str2; // string concatenation
```

➤ Boxing & Unboxing

Boxing and unboxing is a central concept in C#'s type system. It provides a bridge between *value-types* and *reference-types* by permitting any value of a *value-type* to be converted to and from type object. Boxing and unboxing enables a unified view of the type system wherein a value of any type can ultimately be treated as an object.

- **Boxing conversions**

A boxing conversion permits any *value-type* to be implicitly converted to the type object or to any *interface-type* implemented by the *value-type*. Boxing a value of a *value-type* consists of allocating an object instance and copying the *value-type* value into that instance.

The actual process of boxing a value of a *value-type* is best explained by imagining the existence of a **boxing class** for that type. For any *value-type* T, the boxing class would be declared as follows:

```
class T_Box
{
        T value;

        T_Box(T t) {
               value = t;
        }
}
```

Boxing of a value v of type T now consists of executing the expression new T_Box(v), and returning the resulting instance as a value of type object. Thus, the statements

```
int i = 123;
object box = i;
```

conceptually correspond to

```
int i = 123;
object box = new int_Box(i);
```

Boxing classes like T_Box and int_Box above don't actually exist and the dynamic type of a boxed value isn't actually a class type. Instead, a boxed value of type T has the dynamic type T, and a dynamic type check using the is operator can simply reference type T. For example,

```
int i = 123;
object box = i;
if (box is int) {
        Console.Write("Box contains an int");
}
```

will output the string "Box contains an int" on the console.

A boxing conversion implies *making a copy* of the value being boxed. This is different from a conversion of a *reference-type* to type object, in which the value continues to reference the same instance and simply is regarded as the less derived type object. For example, given the declaration

```
struct Point
{
        public int x, y;

        public Point(int x, int y) {
               this.x = x;
               this.y = y;
        }
}
```

the following statements

```
Point p = new Point(10, 10);
object box = p;
p.x = 20;
Console.Write(((Point)box).x);
```

will output the value 10 on the console because the implicit boxing operation that occurs in the assignment of p to box causes the value of p to be copied. Had Point been declared a class instead, the value 20 would be output because p and box would reference the same instance.

- **Unboxing conversions**

An unboxing conversion permits an explicit conversion from type object to any *value-type* or from any *interface-type* to any *value-type* that implements the *interface-type*. An unboxing operation consists of first checking that the object instance is a boxed value of the given *value-type*, and then copying the value out of the instance.

Referring to the imaginary boxing class described in the previous section, an unboxing conversion of an object box to a *value-type* T consists of executing the expression ((T_Box)box).value. Thus, the statements

```
object box = 123;
int i = (int)box;
```

conceptually correspond to

```
object box = new int_Box(123);
int i = ((int_Box)box).value;
```

For an unboxing conversion to a given *value-type* to succeed at run-time, the value of the source operand must be a reference to an object that was previously created by boxing a value of that *value-type*. If the source operand is null or a reference to an incompatible object, a System.InvalidCastException is thrown.

Conditional & Branching Statements

○ **Using the *if* statement**

The *if* statement executes a series of statements if a test Boolean expression evaluates to true.The test expression to evaluate must be Boolean.You cannot use a test numeric expression as in C/C++:

```
int i = 3;
int j = 0;
if ( i > 2 )
{
        j = 3;
}
```

○ **Using the *if-else* statement**

The *if-else* statement adds a path for the false evaluation of the Boolean expression.

```
int i = 3;
int j = 0;
int k = 0;
if ( i > 2 )
```

```
{
        j = 3;
}
else
{
        j = 4;
        k = 5;
}
```

o **Using the *switch case* statement**

The *switch* statement chooses flow of control based on the evaluation of a numeric or string comparison.The *switch* statement does not allow control to fall through to the next case as in C/C++ unless the *case* statement is followed immediately by another *case* statement. In other words, you must use a *break* statement with every case statement.You can also use a *goto* statement, although most programmers frown on using them. Here are two examples:

```
int j = 0;
int i = 1;
switch ( i )
{
        case 1:
                j = 7;
                break;
        case 2:
        case 3:
                j = 22;
                break;
        default:
                j = 33;
                break;
}
```

Looping Statements

o **Using the *for* statement**

C# for loops provide a mechanism for iterating through a loop where you test whether a particular condition holds before you perform another iteration. The syntax is

```
for (initializer; condition; iterator)
        statement(s)
```
where
  o The initializer is the expression evaluated before the first loop is executed (usually initializing a local variable as a loop counter).
  o The condition is the expression checked before each new iteration of the loop (this must evaluate to true for another iteration to be performed).
  o The iterator is an expression evaluated after each iteration (usually incrementing the loop counter).

The *for* statement is used to loop through a series of statements until a test Boolean expression evaluated at the beginning of the loop is false. In the following example, the *WriteLine* method will execute five times:

```
for ( int i = 0; i < 5; i++ )
{
        Console.WriteLine( "I will not talk in class" );
}
```

○ **Using the *while* statement**

The while loop is identical to the while loop in C++ and Java, and the While...Wend loop in Visual Basic. Like the for loop, while is a pretest loop. The syntax is similar, but while loops take only one expression:

```
while(condition){
        statement(s);
}
```

Unlike the for loop, the while loop is most often used to repeat a statement or a block of statements for a number of times that is not known before the loop begins. Usually, a statement inside the while loop ' s body will set a Boolean flag to false on a certain iteration, triggering the end of the loop, as in the following example:

```
bool condition = false;
while (!condition)
{
        // This loop spins until the condition is true.
        DoSomeWork();
        condition = CheckCondition(); // assume CheckCondition() returns a bool
}
```

All of C# ' s looping mechanisms, including the while loop, can forgo the curly braces that follow them if they intend to repeat just a single statement and not a block of statements. Again, many programmers consider it good practice to use braces all of the time.

The following code has the same result as the previous *for* statement example:

```
int i = 0;
while ( i < 5 )
{
        Console.WriteLine( "I will not talk in class" );
        i++;
}
```

○ **Using the *do while* statement**

The do...while loop is the post - test version of the while loop. It does the same thing with the same syntax as do...while in C++ and Java, and the same thing as Loop...While in Visual Basic. This means that the loop ' s test condition is evaluated after the body of the loop has been executed. Consequently, do...while loops are useful for situations in which a block of statements must be executed at least one time, as in this example:

```
bool condition;
do
{
        // This loop will at least execute once, even if Condition is false.
        MustBeCalledAtLeastOnce();
        condition = CheckCondition();
} while (condition);

int i = 6;
do
{
        Console.WriteLine( "I will not talk in class" );
        i++;
}
while ( i < 5 );
```

o **Using the *for each* statement**

The foreach loop is the final C# looping mechanism that we discuss. Whereas the other looping mechanisms were present in the earliest versions of C and C++, the foreach statement is a new addition (borrowed from Visual Basic), and a very welcome one at that. The foreach loop allows you to iterate through each item in a collection. For now, we won't worry about exactly what a collection is; we will just say that it is an object that contains other objects. Technically, to count as a collection, it must support an interface called IEnumerable . Examples of collections include C# arrays, the collection classes in the System.Collection namespaces, and user - defined collection classes. You can get an idea of the syntax of foreach from the following code, if you assume that arrayOfInts is (unsurprisingly) an array of int s:

```
foreach (int temp in arrayOfInts)
{
        Console.WriteLine(temp);
}
```

Here, foreach steps through the array one element at a time. With each element, it places the value of the element in the int variable called temp and then performs an iteration of the loop. Here is another situation where type inference can be used. The foreach loop would become:

```
foreach (var temp in arrayOfInts)
        ...
```

temp would be inferred to int because that is what the collection item type is.

An important point to note with foreach is that you can't change the value of the item in the collection (temp in the preceding code), so code such as the following will not compile:

```
foreach (int temp in arrayOfInts)
{
        temp++;
        Console.WriteLine(temp);
}
```

If you need to iterate through the items in a collection and change their values, you will need to use a for loop instead.

❖ **Jumping Statements**

o **Using the *break* statement**

The *break* statement exits the loop of a *for, while,* or *do while* statement regardless of value of the test Boolean expression. In each of the following examples, the *WriteLine* method will execute two times:

```
int j = 0;
for ( int i = 0; i < 5; i++ )
{
        Console.WriteLine( "I will not talk in class" );
        j++;
        if ( j == 2 )

                break;

}
```

o **Using the *continue* statement**

The *continue* statement will pass flow of control immediately to the start of a loop when encountered. In the following example, "I will not talk in class" will display twice and "At least I'll try not to talk in class" will display three times:

```
int j = 0;
for ( int i = 0; i < 5; i++ )
{
        j++;
        if ( j > 2 )
        {
                Console.WriteLine( "At least I'll try not to talk in class" );
                continue;
        }
        Console.WriteLine( "I will not talk in class" );
}
```

o **Using the *return* statement**

The *return* statement returns flow of control from a method to the caller, optionally passing back a return value. Here is a complete example:

```
using System;
class TestDivision
{
        static void Main(string[] args)
        {
                int dividend = 2;
                int divisor = 0;
                Divider divider = new Divider();
                bool ret = divider.divide(dividend, divisor);
                if ( ret == true )
                        Console.WriteLine("I divided!");
                else
                        Console.WriteLine("Something went horribly wrong!");
        }
}

class Divider
{
        public bool divide( int dividend, int divisor )
        {
                if ( divisor == 0 )
                        return false;
                int result = dividend / divisor;
                return true;
        }
}
```

o **Using the *goto* statement**

The *goto* statement has been the bain of structured programming for many years. C# supports the *goto* statement, although as previously stated, we wouldn't recommend using it.The *goto* statement immediately transfers flow of control to the statement following a label. If you must use *goto*, here is an example:

```
int i = 0;
int j = 0;
while ( i < 5 )
{
        Console.WriteLine( "I will not talk in class" );
        i++;
        j++;
        if ( j == 2 )
                goto jumpeddoutofloop;
}
jumpeddoutofloop:
        Console.WriteLine( "I jumped out" );
```

❖ Array

C# arrays are zero indexed; that is, the array indexes start at zero. Arrays in C# work similarly to how arrays work in most other popular languages There are, however, a few differences that you should be aware of.

When declaring an array, the square brackets ([]) must come after the type, not the identifier. Placing the brackets after the identifier is not legal syntax in C#.

int[] table; // not int table[];

Another detail is that the size of the array is not part of its type as it is in the C language. This allows you to declare an array and assign any array of **int** objects to it, regardless of the array's length.

int[] numbers; // declare numbers as an int array of any size
numbers = new int[10]; // numbers is a 10-element array
numbers = new int[20]; // now it's a 20-element array

o Declaring Arrays

C# supports single-dimensional arrays, multidimensional arrays (rectangular arrays), and array-of-arrays (jagged arrays). The following examples show how to declare different kinds of arrays:

Single-dimensional arrays:

int[] numbers;

Multidimensional arrays:

string[,] names;

Array-of-arrays (jagged):

```
byte[][] scores;
```

Declaring them (as shown above) does not actually create the arrays. In C#, arrays are objects (discussed later in this tutorial) and must be instantiated. The following examples show how to create arrays:

Single-dimensional arrays:

```
int[] numbers = new int[5];
```

Multidimensional arrays:

```
string[,] names = new string[5,4];
```

Array-of-arrays (jagged):

```
byte[][] scores = new byte[5][];
for (int x = 0; x < scores.Length; x++)
{
   scores[x] = new byte[4];
}
```

You can also have larger arrays. For example, you can have a three-dimensional rectangular array:

```
int[,,] buttons = new int[4,5,3];
```

You can even mix rectangular and jagged arrays. For example, the following code declares a single-dimensional array of three-dimensional arrays of two-dimensional arrays of type **int**:

```
int[][,,][,] numbers;
```

Example

The following is a complete C# program that declares and instantiates arrays as discussed above.

```
// arrays.cs
using System;
class DeclareArraysSample
{
   public static void Main()
   {
      // Single-dimensional array
      int[] numbers = new int[5];

      // Multidimensional array
      string[,] names = new string[5,4];
```

```
// Array-of-arrays (jagged array)
byte[][] scores = new byte[5][];

// Create the jagged array
for (int i = 0; i < scores.Length; i++)
{
    scores[i] = new byte[i+3];
}

// Print length of each row
for (int i = 0; i < scores.Length; i++)
{
    Console.WriteLine("Length of row {0} is {1}", i, scores[i].Length);
}
}
}
```

Output

```
Length of row 0 is 3
Length of row 1 is 4
Length of row 2 is 5
Length of row 3 is 6
Length of row 4 is 7
```

○ **Initializing Arrays**

C# provides simple and straightforward ways to initialize arrays at declaration time by enclosing the initial values in curly braces ({}). The following examples show different ways to initialize different kinds of arrays.

Note If you do not initialize an array at the time of declaration, the array members are automatically initialized to the default initial value for the array type. Also, if you declare the array as a field of a type, it will be set to the default value null when you instantiate the type.

Single-Dimensional Array

```
int[] numbers = new int[5] {1, 2, 3, 4, 5};
string[] names = new string[3] {"Matt", "Joanne", "Robert"};
```

You can omit the size of the array, like this:

```
int[] numbers = new int[] {1, 2, 3, 4, 5};
string[] names = new string[] {"Matt", "Joanne", "Robert"};
```

You can also omit the **new** operator if an initializer is provided, like this:

```
int[] numbers = {1, 2, 3, 4, 5};
string[] names = {"Matt", "Joanne", "Robert"};
```

Multidimensional Array

```
int[,] numbers = new int[3, 2] { {1, 2}, {3, 4}, {5, 6} };
string[,] siblings = new string[2, 2] { {"Mike","Amy"}, {"Mary","Albert"} };
```

You can omit the size of the array, like this:

```
int[,] numbers = new int[,] { {1, 2}, {3, 4}, {5, 6} };
string[,] siblings = new string[,] { {"Mike","Amy"}, {"Mary","Albert"} };
```

You can also omit the **new**operator if an initializer is provided, like this:

```
int[,] numbers = { {1, 2}, {3, 4}, {5, 6} };
string[,] siblings = { {"Mike", "Amy"}, {"Mary", "Albert"} };
```

Jagged Array (Array-of-Arrays)

You can initialize jagged arrays like this example:

```
int[][] numbers = new int[2][] { new int[] {2,3,4}, new int[] {5,6,7,8,9} };
```

You can also omit the size of the first array, like this:

```
int[][] numbers = new int[][] { new int[] {2,3,4}, new int[] {5,6,7,8,9} };
```

-or-

```
int[][] numbers = { new int[] {2,3,4}, new int[] {5,6,7,8,9} };
```

Notice that there is no initialization syntax for the elements of a jagged array.

- ○ **Accessing Array Members**

Accessing array members is straightforward and similar to how you access array members in C/C++. For example, the following code creates an array called numbers and then assigns a 5 to the fifth element of the array:

```
int[] numbers = {10, 9, 8, 7, 6, 5, 4, 3, 2, 1, 0};
numbers[4] = 5;
```

The following code declares a multidimensional array and assigns 5 to the member located at [1, 1]:

```
int[,] numbers = { {1, 2}, {3, 4}, {5, 6}, {7, 8}, {9, 10} };
numbers[1, 1] = 5;
```

The following is a declaration of a single-dimension jagged array that contains two elements. The first element is an array of two integers, and the second is an array of three integers:

```
int[][] numbers = new int[][] { new int[] {1, 2}, new int[] {3, 4, 5}
};
```

The following statements assign 58 to the first element of the first array and 667 to the second element of the second array:

```
numbers[0][0] = 58;
numbers[1][1] = 667;
```

o **Arrays are Objects**

In C#, arrays are actually objects. **System.Array** is the abstract base type of all array types. You can use the properties, and other class members, that **System.Array** has. An example of this would be using the Lengthproperty to get the length of an array. The following code assigns the length of the numbers array, which is 5, to a variable called LengthOfNumbers:

```
int[] numbers = {1, 2, 3, 4, 5};
int LengthOfNumbers = numbers.Length;
```

The **System.Array** class provides many other useful methods/properties, such as methods for sorting, searching, and copying arrays.

o **Using foreach on Arrays**

C# also provides the **foreach** statement. This statement provides a simple, clean way to iterate through the elements of an array. For example, the following code creates an array called numbers and iterates through it with the **foreach** statement:

```
int[] numbers = {4, 5, 6, 1, 2, 3, -2, -1, 0};
foreach (int i in numbers)
{
  System.Console.WriteLine(i);
}
```

With multidimensional arrays, you can use the same method to iterate through the elements, for example:

```
int[,] numbers = new int[3, 2] {{9, 99}, {3, 33}, {5, 55}};
foreach(int i in numbers)
{
  Console.Write("{0} ", i);
}
```

The output of this example is:

9 99 3 33 5 55

However, with multidimensional arrays, using a nested **for** loop gives you more control over the array elements.

Understanding the Array Class

The **Array** class, defined in the System namespace, is the base class for arrays in C#. Array class is an abstract base class but it provides CreateInstance method to construct an array. The Array class provides methods for creating, manipulating, searching, and sorting arrays.
Table 1 describes Array class properties.

IsFixedSize	Return a value indicating if an array has a fixed size or not.
IsReadOnly	Returns a value indicating if an array is read-only or not.
IsSynchronized	Returns a value indicating if access to an array is thread-safe or not.
Length	Returns the total number of items in all the dimensions of an array.
Rank	Returns the number of dimensions of an array.
SyncRoot	Returns an object that can be used to synchronize access to the array.

Table 1: The System.Array Class Properties

Table 2 describes some of the Array class methods.

BinarySearch	This method searches a one-dimensional sorted **Array** for a value, using a binary search algorithm.
Clear	This method removes all items of an array and sets a range of items in the array to 0.
Clone	This method creates a shallow copy of the **Array**.
Copy	This method copies a section of one **Array** to another **Array** and performs type casting and boxing as required.
CopyTo	This method copies all the elements of the current one-dimensional **Array** to the specified one-dimensional **Array** starting at the specified destination **Array** index.
CreateInstance	This method initializes a new instance of the **Array** class.
GetEnumerator	This method returns an IEnumerator for the **Array**.
GetLength	This method returns the number of items in an **Array**.
GetLowerBound	This method returns the lower bound of an **Array**.
GetUpperBound	This method returns the upper bound of an **Array**.
GetValue	This method returns the value of the specified item in an Array.
IndexOf	This method returns the index of the first occurrence of a value in a one-dimensional **Array** or in a portion of the **Array**.
Initialize	This method initializes every item of the value-type **Array** by calling the default constructor of the value type.
LastIndexOf	This method returns the index of the last occurrence of a value in a one-dimensional **Array** or in a portion of the **Array**.
Reverse	This method reverses the order of the items in a one-dimensional **Array** or in a portion of the **Array**.
SetValue	This method sets the specified items in the current **Array** to the specified value.
Sort	This method sorts the items in one-dimensional **Array** objects.

Table 2: The System.Array Class Methods

C# Programming Made Easy

The Array Class

Array class is an abstract base class but it provides CreateInstance method to construct an array.
Array names = Array.CreateInstance(typeof(String), 2, 4);
After creating an array using the CreateInstance method, you can use SetValue method to add items to an array. I will discuss SetValue method later in this article.
The Array class provides methods for creating, manipulating, searching, and sorting arrays. Array class provides three boolean properties IsFixedSize, IsReadOnly, and IsSynchronized to see if an array has fixed size, read only or synchronized or not respectively. The Length property of Array class returns the number of items in an array and the Rank property returns number of dimensions in a multi-dimension array.
Listing 1 creates two arrays with a fixed and variable lengths and sends the output to the system console.

```
int [] intArray;
// fixed array with 3 items
intArray = new int[3] {0, 1, 2};
// 2x2 varialbe length array
string[,] names = new string[,] { {"Rosy","Amy"}, {"Peter","Albert"} };
if(intArray.IsFixedSize)
{
Console.WriteLine("Array is fixed size");
Console.WriteLine("Size :" + intArray.Length.ToString());
}
if(names.IsFixedSize)
{
Console.WriteLine("Array is varialbe.");
Console.WriteLine("Size :" + names.Length.ToString());
Console.WriteLine("Rank :" + names.Rank.ToString());
}
```
Listing 1.
Besides these properties, the Array class provides methods to add, insert, delete, copy, binary search, reverse, reverse and so on.

Searching an Item in an Array

The BinarySearch static method of Array class can be used to search for an item in a array. This method uses binary search algorithm to search for an item. The method takes at least two parameters - an array and an object (the item you are looking for). If an item found in an array, the method returns the index of the item (based on first item as 0th item), else method returns a negative value. Listing 2 uses BinarySearch method to search two arrays.

```
int [] intArray = new int[3] {0, 1, 2};
string[] names = new string[] {"Rosy","Amy", "Peter","Albert"};
object obj1 = "Peter";
object obj2 = 1;
int retVal = Array.BinarySearch(names, obj1);
if(retVal >=0)
Console.WriteLine("Item index " +retVal.ToString() );
else
```

```
Console.WriteLine("Item not found");
retVal = Array.BinarySearch(intArray, obj2);
if(retVal >=0)
Console.WriteLine("Item index " +retVal.ToString() );
else
Console.WriteLine("Item not found");
```

Listing 2. Searching an item in a array

Sorting Items in an Array

The Sort static method of the Array class can be used to sort an array items. This method has many overloaded forms. The simplest form takes a parameter of the array, you want to sort to. Listing 3 uses Sort method to sort an array items.

```
string[] names = new string[] {"Rosy","Amy", "Peter","Albert"};
Console.WriteLine("Original Array:");
foreach (string str in names)
{
Console.WriteLine(str);
}
Console.WriteLine("Sorted Array:");
Array.Sort(names);
foreach (string str in names)
{
Console.WriteLine(str);
}
```

Listing 3. Sorting an array items

Getting and Setting Values

The GetValue and SetValue methods of the Array class can be used to return a value from an index of an array and set values of an array item at a specified index respectively. The code listed in Listing 4 creates a 2-dimension array instance using the CreateInstance method. After that I use SetValue method to add values to the array.

In the end I find number of items in both dimensions and use GetValue method to read values and display on the console.

```
Array names = Array.CreateInstance( typeof(String), 2, 4 );
names.SetValue( "Rosy", 0, 0 );
names.SetValue( "Amy", 0, 1 );
names.SetValue( "Peter", 0, 2 );
names.SetValue( "Albert", 0, 3 );
names.SetValue( "Mel", 1, 0 );
names.SetValue( "Mongee", 1, 1 );
names.SetValue( "Luma", 1, 2 );
```

```
names.SetValue( "Lara", 1, 3 );
int items1 = names.GetLength(0);
int items2 = names.GetLength(1);
for ( int i =0; i < items1; i++ )
for ( int j = 0; j < items2; j++ )
Console.WriteLine(i.ToString() +","+ j.ToString() +": " +names.GetValue( i, j ) );
```

Listing 4. Using GetValue and SetValue methods

Other Methods of Array Class

The Reverse static method of the Array class reverses the order of items in a array. Similar to the sort method, you can just pass an array as a parameter of the Reverse method.

```
Array.Reverse(names);
```

The Clear static method of the Array class removes all items of an array and sets its length to zero. This method takes three parameters - first an array object, second starting index of the array and third is number of elements. The following code removes two elements from the array starting at index 1 (means second element of the array).

```
Array.Clear(names, 1, 2);
```

The GetLength method returns the number of items in an array. The GetLowerBound and GetUppperBound methods return the lower and upper bounds of an array respectively. All these three methods take at least a parameter, which is the index of the dimension of an array. The following code snippet uses all three methods.

```
string[] names = new string[] {"Rosy","Amy", "Peter","Albert"};
Console.WriteLine(names.GetLength(0).ToString());
Console.WriteLine(names.GetLowerBound(0).ToString());
Console.WriteLine(names.GetUpperBound(0).ToString());
```

The Copy static method of the Array class copies a section of an array to another array. The CopyTo method copies all the elements of an array to another one-dimension array. The code listed in Listing 5 copies contents of an integer array to an array of object types.

```
// Creates and initializes a new Array of type Int32.
Array oddArray = Array.CreateInstance( Type.GetType("System.Int32"), 5 );
oddArray.SetValue(1, 0);
oddArray.SetValue(3, 1);
oddArray.SetValue(5, 2);
oddArray.SetValue(7, 3);
oddArray.SetValue(9, 4);
// Creates and initializes a new Array of type Object.
Array objArray = Array.CreateInstance( Type.GetType("System.Object"), 5 );
Array.Copy(oddArray, oddArray.GetLowerBound(0), objArray, objArray.GetLowerBound(0), 4 );
int items1 = objArray.GetUpperBound(0);
```

```
for ( int i =0; i < items1; i++ )
Console.WriteLine(objArray.GetValue(i).ToString());
```

Listing 5. Copying an array.
You can even copy a part of an array to another array by passing number of items and starting item in the Copy method. The following format copies a range of items from an Array starting at the specified source index and pastes them to another **Array** starting at the specified destination index.

```
public static void Copy(Array, int, Array, int, int);
```

❖ Struct

Struct is an encapsulated entity. Struct doesn't uses complete oops concept but are used for user defined data type. All the member of the struct has to be initialized, as it is value type.

A struct is a simple user-defined type, a lightweight alternative to a class. A structure in C# is simply a composite data type consisting of a number elements of other types.

Similar to classes, structures have behaviors and attributes. As a value type, structures directly contain their value so their object or instance is stored on the stack.

Struts support access modifiers, constructors, indexers, methods, fields, nested types, operators, and properties.

How do define struct?

```
public struct Student

{

    int id;

    int zipcode;

    double salary;

}
```

Note: struct members may not be declared protected.

Structs are simple to use and can prove to be useful at times. Just keep in mind that they're created on the stack and that you're not dealing with references to them but dealing directly with them. Whenever you have a need for a type that will be used often and is mostly just a piece of data, structs might be a good option.

Practical demonstration of struct

```
using System;

namespace example_struct

{

  class Program
```

```csharp
{
    public struct Student
    {
        int id;
        int zipcode;
        double salary;
        // all the members of the struct has to be initialized in this way
        public Student(int id, int zipcode, double salary)
        {
            this.id = id;
            this.zipcode = zipcode;
            this.salary = salary;
        }
        // all the members of the struct has to be initialized either in this way
        public Student(int id, int zipcode)
        {
            this.id = id;
            this.zipcode = zipcode;
            this.salary = 3400.00;
        }
        // if you left any member of a struct uninitialzed it will give error
        // code below will give error because the zipcode and salary field is left uninitialzed
        //public Student(int id)
        //{
        //    this.id = id;
        //}
        // struct can also have copy constructor but have to be fully initialzed
        public Student(Student x)
        {
            this.id = x.id;
            this.zipcode = x.zipcode;
```

```
        this.salary = x.salary;

    }

    public void DisplayValues()

    {

        Console.WriteLine("ID: " + this.id.ToString());

        Console.WriteLine("Zipcode : " + this.zipcode.ToString());

        Console.WriteLine("Salary : " + this.salary.ToString());

    }

}

static void Main(string[] args)

{

    Student stu = new Student(12, 201301, 4560.00);

    Student stu1 = new Student(stu);

    stu.DisplayValues();

    Console.WriteLine("Copy constructor values");

    stu1.DisplayValues();

    Console.ReadLine();

    }

  }

}
```

Some points about structs

- Struct is used to improve the performance and clarity of code.
- Struct uses fewer resources in memory than class.
- When we have small and frequent use of some work use structs over classes.
- Performance can suffer when using structures in situations where reference types are expected due to boxing and unboxing.
- You should pass structs to method as ref parameters in order to avoid the performance loss associated with copying data.
- Structs reside on the stack, so we should keep them small.
- Structs can't be inherited and we can say they are sealed.
- Structure implicitly inherits from System.ValueType.
- The default constructor of a structure initializes each field to a default value. You cannot replace the default constructor of a structure.
- You can't define destructor for structs
- Structs can be inherited from an interface?
-

C# Programming Made Easy

Practical program showing that struct and inherit from an interface:

```csharp
using System;

using System.Collections.Generic;

using System.Linq;

using System.Text;

namespace example_struct_using_interface
{
    class Program
    {
        public interface aa
        {
            // no access specifier is given in interface methods (by defualt they are public)
            double Increment();
            void DisplayValues();
        }


        public struct Student : aa
        {
            int id;
            int zipcode;
            double salary;
            public Student(int id, int zipcode, double salary)
            {
                this.id = id;
                this.zipcode = zipcode;
                this.salary = salary;
            }
            public void DisplayValues()
            {
                Console.WriteLine("ID: " + this.id.ToString());
                Console.WriteLine("Zipcode : " + this.zipcode.ToString());
```

```
      Console.WriteLine("Salary : " + this.salary.ToString());

   }

   public double Increment()

   {

      return(this.salary += 1000.00);

   }

}

   static void Main(string[] args)

   {

      Student stu = new Student(12, 201301, 4560.00);

      stu.DisplayValues();

      Console.WriteLine("Salary after increment is {0}", stu.Increment());

      Console.ReadLine();

   }

  }

}
```

Structs and inheritance

Structs don't provide inheritance. It is not possible to inherit from a struct and a struct can't derive from any class.

Once exception that all type in C# is derive from the class System.Object, so structs also have the access to the methods etc., of System.Object.

Note: Inheritance is indirect: Structs derive from System.ValueType, which in turns derive from System.Object.ValueType adds no new method of its own, but provides overrides of some the Object methods that are more appropriate to value types.

Difference between structs and classes

structs	classes
• structs are value type	• classes are reference type
• structs are stored in stack or a inline	• classes are stored on managed heap
• structs doesn't support inheritance	• classes support inheritance
• But handing of constructor is different in structs. The complier supplies a default no-parameter constructor, which your are	• Constructors are fully supported in classes

not permitted to replace

Keep you knowledge base upgraded. Hope the article would have helped you in understanding structs and their usage. Your feedback and constructive contributions are welcome. Please feel free to contact me for feedback or comments you may have about this article.

❖ Classes

A class is a data structure that may contain data members (constants and fields), function members (methods, properties, indexers, events, operators, instance constructors, static constructors, and destructors), and nested types. Class types support inheritance, a mechanism whereby a derived class can extend and specialize a base class.

→ Class declarations

A *class-declaration* is a *type-declaration* that declares a new class.

> *class-declaration:*
>   *attributes$_{opt}$ class-modifiers$_{opt}$* class *identifier class-base$_{opt}$ class-body* ;$_{opt}$

A *class-declaration* consists of an optional set of *attributes*, followed by an optional set of *class-modifiers*, followed by the keyword class and an *identifier* that names the class, followed by an optional *class-base* specification, followed by a *class-body*, optionally followed by a semicolon.

→ Class modifiers

A *class-declaration* may optionally include a sequence of class modifiers:

> *class-modifiers:*
>   *class-modifier*
>   *class-modifiers class-modifier*
>
> *class-modifier:*
>   new
>   public
>   protected
>   internal
>   private
>   abstract
>   sealed

> It is an error for the same modifier to appear multiple times in a class declaration.

The new modifier is only permitted on nested classes. It specifies that the class hides an inherited member by the same name.

The public, protected, internal, and private modifiers control the accessibility of the class. Depending on the context in which the class declaration occurs, some of these modifiers may not be permitted

Abstract classes

The abstract modifier is used to indicate that a class is incomplete and that it is intended to be used only as a base class. An abstract class differs from a non-abstract class is the following ways:

An abstract class cannot be instantiated directly, and it is an error to use the new operator on an abstract class. While it is possible to have variables and values whose compile-time types are abstract, such variables and values will necessarily either be null or contain references to instances of non-abstract classes derived from the abstract types.

An abstract class is permitted (but not required) to contain abstract members.

An abstract class cannot be sealed.

When a non-abstract class is derived from an abstract class, the non-abstract class must include actual implementations of all inherited abstract members. Such implementations are provided by overriding the abstract members. In the example

```
abstract class A
{
    public abstract void F();
}
abstract class B: A
{
    public void G() {}
}
class C: B
{
    public override void F() {
        // actual implementation of F
    }
}
```

the abstract class A introduces an abstract method F. Class B introduces an additional method G, but since it doesn't provide an implementation of F, B must also be declared abstract. Class C overrides F and provides an actual implementation. Since there are no abstract members in C, C is permitted (but not required) to be non-abstract.

Sealed classes

The sealed modifier is used to prevent derivation from a class. An error occurs if a sealed class is specified as the base class of another class.

A sealed class cannot also be an abstract class.

The sealed modifier is primarily used to prevent unintended derivation, but it also enables certain run-time optimizations. In particular, because a sealed class is known to never have any derived classes, it is possible to transform virtual function member invocations on sealed class instances into non-virtual invocations.

Class members

The members of a class consist of the members introduced by its *class-member-declaration*s and the members inherited from the direct base class.

class-member-declarations:
    class-member-declaration
    class-member-declarations *class-member-declaration*

```
class-member-declaration:
    constant-declaration
    field-declaration
    method-declaration
    property-declaration
    event-declaration
    indexer-declaration
    operator-declaration


    constructor-declaration
    destructor-declaration
    static-constructor-declaration
    type-declaration
```

The members of a class are divided into the following categories:

Constants, which represent constant values associated with the class.

Fields, which are the variables of the class.

Methods, which implement the computations and actions that can be performed by the class.

Properties, which define named attributes and the actions associated with reading and writing those attributes.

Events, which define notifications that can be generated by the class.

Indexers, which permit instances of the class to be indexed in the same way as arrays.

Operators, which define the expression operators that can be applied to instances of the class.

Instance constructors, which implement the actions required to initialize instances of the class.

Destructors, which implement the actions to be performed before instances of the class are permanently discarded.

Static constructors, which implement the actions required to initialize the class itself.

Types, which represent the types that are local to the class.

Members that can contain executable code are collectively known as the *function members* of the class.

A *class-declaration* creates a new declaration space, and the *class-member-declarations* immediately contained by the *class-declaration* introduce new members into this declaration space. The following rules apply to *class-member-declaration*s:

Instance constructors, static constructors and destructors must have the same name as the immediately enclosing class. All other members must have names that differ from the name of the immediately enclosing class.

The name of a constant, field, property, event, or type must differ from the names of all other members declared in the same class.

The name of a method must differ from the names of all other non-methods declared in the same class. In addition, the signature of a method must differ from the signatures of all other methods declared in the same class.

The signature of an instance constructor must differ from the signatures of all other instance constructors declared in the same class.

The signature of an indexer must differ from the signatures of all other indexers declared in the same class.

The signature of an operator must differ from the signatures of all other operators declared in the same class.

The inherited members of a class are not part of the declaration space of a class. Thus, a derived class is allowed to declare a member with the same name or signature as an inherited member (which in effect hides the inherited member).

Inheritance

A class *inherits* the members of its direct base class. Inheritance means that a class implicitly contains all members of its direct base class, except for the instance constructors, static constructors, and destructors of the base class. Some important aspects of inheritance are:

Inheritance is transitive. If C is derived from B, and B is derived from A, then C inherits the members declared in B as well as the members declared in A.

A derived class *extends* its direct base class. A derived class can add new members to those it inherits, but it cannot remove the definition of an inherited member.

Instance constructors, static constructors, and destructors are not inherited, but all other members are, regardless of their declared accessibility. However, depending on their declared accessibility, inherited members might not be accessible in a derived class.

A derived class can *hide* inherited members by declaring new members with the same name or signature. Note however that hiding an inherited member does not remove the member—it merely makes the member inaccessible in the derived class.

An instance of a class contains a set of all instance fields declared in the class and its base classes, and an implicit conversion exists from a derived class type to any of its base class types. Thus, a reference to an instance of some derived class can be treated as a reference to an instance of any of its base classes.

A class can declare virtual methods, properties, and indexers, and derived classes can override the implementation of these function members. This enables classes to exhibit polymorphic behavior wherein the actions performed by a function member invocation vary depending on the run-time type of the instance through which the function member is invoked.

Static and instance members

Members of a class are either *static members* or *instance members*. Generally speaking, it is useful to think of static members as belonging to classes and instance members as belonging to objects (instances of classes).

When a field, method, property, event, operator, or constructor declaration includes a static modifier, it declares a static member. In addition, a constant or type declaration implicitly declares a static member. Static members have the following characteristics:

When a static member is referenced in a *member-access* of the form E.M, E must denote a type that has a member M. It is an error for E to denote an instance.

A static field identifies exactly one storage location. No matter how many instances of a class are created, there is only ever one copy of a static field.

A static function member does not operate on a specific instance, and it is an error to refer to this in such a function member.

When a field, method, property, event, indexer, constructor, or destructor declaration does not include a static modifier, it declares an instance member. (An instance member is sometimes called a non-static member.) Instance members have the following characteristics:

When an instance member is referenced in a *member-access* of the form E.M, E must denote an instance of a type that has a member M. It is an error for E to denote a type.

Every instance of a class contains a separate set of all instance fields of the class.

An instance function member operates on a given instance of the class, and this instance can be accessed as this.

The following example illustrates the rules for accessing static and instance members:

```
class Test
{
    int x;
    static int y;
    void F() {
        x = 1;          // Ok, same as this.x = 1
        y = 1;          // Ok, same as Test.y = 1
    }
    static void G() {
        x = 1;          // Error, cannot access this.x
        y = 1;          // Ok, same as Test.y = 1
    }
    static void Main() {
        Test t = new Test();
        t.x = 1;            // Ok
        t.y = 1;            // Error, cannot access static member through
instance
        Test.x = 1;         // Error, cannot access instance member through
type
        Test.y = 1;         // Ok
    }
}
```

The F method shows that in an instance function member, a *simple-name* (§**Error! Reference source not found.**) can be used to access both instance members and static members. The G method shows that in a static function member, it is an error to access an instance member through a *simple-name*. The Main method shows that in a *member-access* (§**Error! Reference source not found.**), instance members must be accessed through instances, and static members must be accessed through types.

Fields

A *field* is a member that represents a variable associated with an object or class. A *field-declaration* introduces one or more fields of a given type.

field-declaration:
    attributes_{opt} field-modifiers_{opt} type variable-declarators ;

field-modifiers:
    field-modifier
    field-modifiers field-modifier

field-modifier:
  new
  public
  protected
  internal
  private
  static
  readonly
  volatile

variable-declarators:
  variable-declarator
  variable-declarators , variable-declarator

variable-declarator:
  identifier
  identifier = variable-initializer

variable-initializer:
  expression
  array-initializer

A *field-declaration* may include a set of *attributes*, a new modifier, a valid combination of the four access modifiers, a static modifier. In addition, a *field-declaration* may include a readonly modifier or a volatile modifier but not both. The attributes and modifiers apply to all of the members declared by the *field-declaration*.

The *type* of a *field-declaration* specifies the type of the members introduced by the declaration. The type is followed by a list of *variable-declarators*, each of which introduces a new member. A *variable-declarator* consists of an *identifier* that names the member, optionally followed by an "=" token and a *variable-initializer* that gives the initial value of the member.

The *type* of a field must be at least as accessible as the field itself. The value of a field is obtained in an expression using a *simple-name* or a *member-access*. The value of a non-read only field is modified using an *assignment*. The value of a non-read only field can be both obtained and modified using postfix increment and decrement operators and prefix increment and decrement operators.

A field declaration that declares multiple fields is equivalent to multiple declarations of single fields with the same attributes, modifiers, and type. For example

```
class A
{
    public static int X = 1, Y, Z = 100;
}
```
is equivalent to

```
class A
{
    public static int X = 1;
    public static int Y;
    public static int Z = 100;
}
```

Static and instance fields

When a *field-declaration* includes a static modifier, the fields introduced by the declaration are **static fields**. When no static modifier is present, the fields introduced by the declaration are *instance fields.* Static fields and instance fields are two of the several kinds of variables supported by C#, and are at times referred to as **static variables** and **instance variables**.

A static field identifies exactly one storage location. No matter how many instances of a class are created, there is only ever one copy of a static field. A static field comes into existence when the type in which it is declared is loaded, and ceases to exist when the type in which it is declared is unloaded.

Every instance of a class contains a separate set of all instance fields of the class. An instance field comes into existence when a new instance of its class is created, and ceases to exist when there are no references to that instance and the destructor of the instance has executed.

When a field is referenced in a *member-access* of the form E.M, if M is a static field, E must denote a type that has a field M, and if M is an instance field, E must denote an instance of a type that has a field M.

Readonly fields

When a *field-declaration* includes a readonly modifier, the fields introduced by the declaration are **readonly fields**. Direct assignments to readonly fields can only occur as part of the declaration or in an instance constructor (for readonly non-static fields) or static constructor (for readonly static fields) in the same class. (A readonly field can be assigned multiple times in these contexts.) Specifically, direct assignments to a readonly field are permitted only in the following contexts:

In the *variable-declarator* that introduces the field (by including a *variable-initializer* in the declaration).

For an instance field, in the instance constructors of the class that contains the field declaration, or for a static field, in the static constructor of the class that contains the field declaration. These are also the only contexts in which it is valid to pass a readonly field as an out or ref parameter.

Attempting to assign to a readonly field or pass it as an out or ref parameter in any other context is an error.

Using static readonly fields for constants

A static readonly field is useful when a symbolic name for a constant value is desired, but when the type of the value is not permitted in a const declaration, or when the value cannot be computed at compile-time. In the example

```
public class Color
{
    public static readonly Color Black = new Color(0, 0, 0);
    public static readonly Color White = new Color(255, 255, 255);
    public static readonly Color Red = new Color(255, 0, 0);
    public static readonly Color Green = new Color(0, 255, 0);
    public static readonly Color Blue = new Color(0, 0, 255);

    private byte red, green, blue;

    public Color(byte r, byte g, byte b) {
        red = r;
        green = g;
        blue = b;
    }
}
```

the Black, White, Red, Green, and Blue members cannot be declared as const members because their values cannot be computed at compile-time. However, declaring them as static readonly fields instead has much the same effect.

Methods

A *method* is a member that implements a computation or action that can be performed by an object or class. Methods are declared using *method-declaration*s:

> *method-declaration:*
>   *method-header   method-body*

> *method-header:*
>   *attributes$_{opt}$ method-modifiers$_{opt}$ return-type   member-name   (formal-parameter-list$_{opt}$)*

> *method-modifiers:*
>   *method-modifier*
>   *method-modifiers   method-modifier*

> *method-modifier:*
>   new
>   public
>   protected
>   internal
>   private
>   static
>   virtual
>   sealed
>   override
>   abstract
>   extern

> *return-type:*
>   *type*
>   void

> *member-name:*
>   *identifier*
>   *interface-type   .   identifier*

> *method-body:*
>   *block*
>   ;

A *method-declaration* may include a set of *attributes*, a new modifier, an extern modifier, a valid combination of the four access modifiers, and a valid combination of the static, virtual, override, and abstract modifiers. In addition, a method that includes the override modifier may also include the sealed modifier

The static, virtual, override and abstract modifiers are mutually exclusive except in one case. The abstract and override modifiers may be used together so that an abstract method can override a virtual one.

The *return-type* of a method declaration specifies the type of the value computed and returned by the method. The *return-type* is void if the method does not return a value.

The *member-name* specifies the name of the method. Unless the method is an explicit interface member implementation, the *member-name* is simply an *identifier*. For an explicit interface member implementation, the *member-name* consists of an *interface-type* followed by a "." and an *identifier*.

The optional *formal-parameter-list* specifies the parameters of the method. The *return-type* and each of the types referenced in the *formal-parameter-list* of a method must be at least as accessible as the method itself.

For abstract and extern methods, the *method-body* consists simply of a semicolon. For all other methods, the *method-body* consists of a *block* which specifies the statements to execute when the method is invoked.

The name and the formal parameter list of a method define the signature of the method. Specifically, the signature of a method consists of its name and the number, modifiers, and types of its formal parameters. The return type is not part of a method's signature, nor is the names of the formal parameters.

The name of a method must differ from the names of all other non-methods declared in the same class. In addition, the signature of a method must differ from the signatures of all other methods declared in the same class.

→ Method parameters

The parameters of a method, if any, are declared by the method's *formal-parameter-list*.

 formal-parameter-list:
  fixed-parameters
  fixed-parameters   ,   *parameter-array*
  parameter-array

 fixed-parameters:
  fixed-parameter
  fixed-parameters , *fixed-parameter*

 fixed-parameter:
  attributes$_{opt}$ *parameter-modifier*$_{opt}$ *type* *identifier*

 parameter-modifier:
  ref
  out

 parameter-array:
  attributes$_{opt}$ params *array-type* *identifier*

The formal parameter list consists of one or more comma-separated parameters of which only the last may be a *parameter-array*.

A *fixed-parameter* consists of an optional set of *attributes*, an optional ref or out modifier, a *type*, and an *identifier*. Each *fixed-parameter* declares a parameter of the given type with the given name.

A *parameter-array* consists of an optional set of *attributes*, a params modifier, an *array-type*, and an *identifier*. A parameter array declares a single parameter of the given array type with the given name. The *array-type* of a parameter array must be a single-dimensional array type. In a method invocation, a parameter array permits either a single argument of the given array type to be specified, or it permits zero or more arguments of the array element type to be specified.

A method declaration creates a separate declaration space for parameters and local variables. Names are introduced into this declaration space by the formal parameter list of the method and by local variable declarations in the *block* of the method. All names in the declaration space of a method must be unique. Thus, it is an error for a parameter or local variable to have the same name as another parameter or local variable.

There are four kinds of formal parameters:

Value parameters, which are declared without any modifiers.

Reference parameters, which are declared with the ref modifier.

Output parameters, which are declared with the out modifier.

Parameter arrays, which are declared with the params modifier.

As described in §**Error! Reference source not found.**, the ref and out modifiers are part of a method's signature, but the params modifier is not.

→ *Value parameters*

A parameter declared with no modifiers is a value parameter. A value parameter corresponds to a local variable that gets its initial value from the corresponding argument supplied in the method invocation.

When a formal parameter is a value parameter, the corresponding argument in a method invocation must be an expression of a type that is implicitly convertible to the formal parameter type.

A method is permitted to assign new values to a value parameter. Such assignments only affect the local storage location represented by the value parameter—they have no effect on the actual argument given in the method invocation.

→ *Reference parameters*

A parameter declared with a ref modifier is a reference parameter. Unlike a value parameter, a reference parameter does not create a new storage location. Instead, a reference parameter represents the same storage location as the variable given as the argument in the method invocation.

When a formal parameter is a reference parameter, the corresponding argument in a method invocation must consist of the keyword ref followed by a *variable-reference* of the same type as the formal parameter. A variable must be definitely assigned before it can be passed as a reference parameter.

Within a method, a reference parameter is always considered definitely assigned.

The example

```
class Test
{
    static void Swap(ref int x, ref int y) {
        int temp = x;
        x = y;
        y = temp;
    }
```

```
static void Main() {
        int i = 1, j = 2;
        Swap(ref i, ref j);
        Console.WriteLine("i = {0}, j = {1}", i, j);
    }
}
```

produces the output

i = 2, j = 1

For the invocation of Swap in Main, x represents i and y represents j. Thus, the invocation has the effect of swapping the values of i and j.

In a method that takes reference parameters it is possible for multiple names to represent the same storage location. In the example

```
class A
{
    string s;
    void F(ref string a, ref string b) {
            s = "One";
            a = "Two";
            b = "Three";
    }
    void G() {
            F(ref s, ref s);
    }
}
```

the invocation of F in G passes a reference to s for both a and b. Thus, for that invocation, the names s, a, and b all refer to the same storage location, and the three assignments all modify the instance field s.

→ *Output parameters*

A parameter declared with an out modifier is an output parameter. Similar to a reference parameter, an output parameter does not create a new storage location. Instead, an output parameter represents the same storage location as the variable given as the argument in the method invocation.

When a formal parameter is an output parameter, the corresponding argument in a method invocation must consist of the keyword out followed by a *variable-reference* of the same type as the formal parameter. A variable need not be definitely assigned before it can be passed as an output parameter, but following an invocation where a variable was passed as an output parameter, the variable is considered definitely assigned.

Within a method, just like a local variable, an output parameter is initially considered unassigned and must be definitely assigned before its value is used.

Every output parameter of a method must be definitely assigned before the method returns.

Output parameters are typically used in methods that produce multiple return values. For example:

```
class Test
{
    static void SplitPath(string path, out string dir, out string name) {
        int i = path.Length;
        while (i > 0) {
            char ch = path[i – 1];
            if (ch == '\\' || ch == '/' || ch == ':') break;
            i--;
        }
        dir = path.Substring(0, i);
        name = path.Substring(i);
    }
    static void Main() {
        string dir, name;
        SplitPath("c:\\Windows\\System\\hello.txt", out dir, out name);
        Console.WriteLine(dir);
        Console.WriteLine(name);
    }
}
```

The example produces the output:

```
c:\Windows\System\
hello.txt
```

Note that the dir and name variables can be unassigned before they are passed to SplitPath, and that they are considered definitely assigned following the call.

→ *Parameter arrays*

A parameter declared with a params modifier is a parameter array. If a formal parameter list includes a parameter array, it must be the right-most parameter in the list and it must be of a single-dimensional array type. For example, the types string[] and string[][] can be used as the type of a parameter array, but the type string[,] can not. It is not possible to combine the params modifier with the ref and out modifiers.

A parameter array permits arguments to be specified in one of two ways in a method invocation:

The argument given for a parameter array can be a single expression of a type that is implicitly convertible (§**Error! Reference source not found.**) to the parameter array type. In this case, the parameter array acts precisely like a value parameter.

Alternatively, the invocation can specify zero or more arguments for the parameter array, where each argument is an expression of a type that is implicitly convertible (§**Error! Reference source not found.**) to the element type of the parameter array. In this case, the invocation creates an instance of the parameter array type with a length corresponding to the number of arguments, initializes the elements of the array instance with the given argument values, and uses the newly created array instance as the actual argument.

Except for allowing a variable number of arguments in an invocation, a parameter array is precisely equivalent to a value parameter (§0) of the same type.

The example

```
class Test
{
    static void F(params int[] args) {
        Console.WriteLine("Array contains {0} elements:", args.Length);
        foreach (int i in args) Console.Write(" {0}", i);
                Console.WriteLine();
    }

    static void Main() {
        int[] arr = {1, 2, 3};
        F(a);
        F(10, 20, 30, 40);
        F();
    }
}
```

produces the output

```
Array contains 3 elements: 1 2 3
Array contains 4 elements: 10 20 30 40
Array contains 0 elements:
```

The first invocation of F simply passes the array a as a value parameter. The second invocation of F automatically creates a four-element int[] with the given element values and passes that array instance as a value parameter. Likewise, the third invocation of F creates a zero-element int[] and passes that instance as a value parameter. The second and third invocations are precisely equivalent to writing:

```
F(new int[] {10, 20, 30, 40});
F(new int[] {});
```

When performing overload resolution, a method with a parameter array may be applicable either in its normal form or in its expanded form (§**Error! Reference source not found.**). The expanded form of a method is available only if the normal form of the method is not applicable and only if a method with the same signature as the expanded form is not already declared in the same type.

The example

```
class Test
{
    static void F(params object[] a) {
        Console.WriteLine("F(object[])");
    }

    static void F() {
        Console.WriteLine("F()");
    }

    static void F(object a0, object a1) {
        Console.WriteLine("F(object,object)");
    }

    static void Main() {
        F();
        F(1);
        F(1, 2);
        F(1, 2, 3);
        F(1, 2, 3, 4);
    }
}
```

produces the output

```
F();
F(object[]);
F(object,object);
F(object[]);
F(object[]);
```

The example

```
class Test
{
    static void F(params object[] args) {
        foreach (object o in a) {
            Console.Write(o.GetType().FullName);
            Console.Write(" ");
        }
        Console.WriteLine();
    }
    static void Main() {
        object[] a = {1, "Hello", 123.456};
        object o = a;
        F(a);
        F((object)a);
        F(o);
        F((object[])o);
    }
}
```

produces the output

```
System.Int32 System.String System.Double
System.Object[]
System.Object[]
System.Int32 System.String System.Double
```

Static and instance methods

When a method declaration includes a static modifier, the method is said to be a static method. When no static modifier is present, the method is said to be an instance method.

A static method does not operate on a specific instance, and it is an error to refer to this in a static method. Furthermore, it is an error for a static method to include any of the following modifiers: virtual, abstract, or override.

An instance method operates on a given instance of a class, and this instance can be accessed as this.

Virtual methods

When an instance method declaration includes a virtual modifier, the method is said to be a virtual method. When no virtual modifier is present, the method is said to be a non-virtual method.

It is an error for a method declaration that includes the virtual modifier to include any of the following modifiers: static, abstract, or override.

The implementation of a non-virtual method is invariant: The implementation is the same whether the method is invoked on an instance of the class in which it is declared or an instance of a derived class. In contrast, the implementation of a virtual method can be superseded by derived classes. The process of superseding the implementation of an inherited virtual method is known as **overriding** the method.

In a virtual method invocation, the **run-time type** of the instance for which the invocation takes place determines the actual method implementation to invoke. In a non-virtual method invocation, the **compile-time type** of the instance is the determining factor. In precise terms, when a method named N is invoked with an argument list A on an instance with a compile-time type C and a run-time type R (where R is either C or a class derived from C), the invocation is processed as follows:

First, overload resolution is applied to C, N, and A, to select a specific method M from the set of methods declared in and inherited by C.

Then, if M is a non-virtual method, M is invoked.

Otherwise, M is a virtual method, and the most derived implementation of M with respect to R is invoked.

For every virtual method declared in or inherited by a class, there exists a **most derived implementation** of the method with respect to that class. The most derived implementation of a virtual method M with respect to a class R is determined as follows:

If R contains the introducing virtual declaration of M, then this is the most derived implementation of M.

Otherwise, if R contains an override of M, then this is the most derived implementation of M.

Otherwise, the most derived implementation of M is the same as that of the direct base class of R.

The following example illustrates the differences between virtual and non-virtual methods:

```
class A
{
    public void F() { Console.WriteLine("A.F"); }
    public virtual void G() { Console.WriteLine("A.G"); }
}
class B: A
{
    new public void F() { Console.WriteLine("B.F"); }
    public override void G() { Console.WriteLine("B.G"); }
}
class Test
{
    static void Main() {
        B b = new B();
        A a = b;
        a.F();
        b.F();
        a.G();
        b.G();
    }
}
```

In the example, A introduces a non-virtual method F and a virtual method G. The class B introduces a *new* non-virtual method F, thus *hiding* the inherited F, and also *overrides* the inherited method G. The example produces the output:

A.F
B.F
B.G
B.G

Notice that the statement a.G() invokes B.G, not A.G. This is because the run-time type of the instance (which is B), not the compile-time type of the instance (which is A), determines the actual method implementation to invoke.

Because methods are allowed to hide inherited methods, it is possible for a class to contain several virtual methods with the same signature. This does not present an ambiguity problem, since all but the most derived method are hidden. In the example

```
class A
{
    public virtual void F() { Console.WriteLine("A.F"); }
}

class B: A
{
    public override void F() { Console.WriteLine("B.F"); }
}

class C: B
{
    new public virtual void F() { Console.WriteLine("C.F"); }
}

class D: C
{
    public override void F() { Console.WriteLine("D.F"); }
}

class Test
{
    static void Main() {
        D d = new D();
        A a = d;
        B b = d;
        C c = d;
        a.F();
        b.F();
        c.F();
        d.F();
    }
}
```

the C and D classes contain two virtual methods with the same signature: The one introduced by A and the one introduced by C. The method introduced by C hides the method inherited from A. Thus, the override declaration in D overrides the method introduced by C, and it is not possible for D to override the method introduced by A. The example produces the output:

B.F
B.F
D.F
D.F

Note that it is possible to invoke the hidden virtual method by accessing an instance of D through a less derived type in which the method is not hidden.

Override methods

When an instance method declaration includes an override modifier, the method is said to be an *override method*. An override method overrides an inherited virtual method with the same signature. Whereas a virtual method declaration *introduces* a new method, an override method declaration *specializes* an existing inherited virtual method by providing a new implementation of the method.

It is an error for an override method declaration to include any of the following modifiers: new, static, or virtual. An override method declaration may include the abstract modifier. This enables a virtual method to be overridden by an abstract method.

The method overridden by an override declaration is known as the *overridden base method*. For an override method M declared in a class C, the overridden base method is determined by examining each base class of C, starting with the direct base class of C and continuing with each successive direct base class, until an accessible method with the same signature as M is located. For the purposes of locating the overridden base method, a method is considered accessible if it is public, if it is protected, if it is protected internal, or if it is internal and declared in the same program as C.

A compile-time error occurs unless all of the following are true for an override declaration:

An overridden base method can be located as described above.

The overridden base method is a virtual, abstract, or override method. In other words, the overridden base method cannot be static or non-virtual.

The overridden base method is not a sealed method.

The override declaration and the overridden base method have the same declared accessibility. In other words, an override declaration cannot change the accessibility of the virtual method.

An override declaration can access the overridden base method using a *base-access*. In the example

```csharp
class A
{
    int x;
    public virtual void PrintFields() {
        Console.WriteLine("x = {0}", x);
    }
}
class B: A
{
    int y;
    public override void PrintFields() {
        base.PrintFields();
        Console.WriteLine("y = {0}", y);
    }
}
```

the base.PrintFields() invocation in B invokes the PrintFields method declared in A. A *base-access* disables the virtual invocation mechanism and simply treats the base method as a non-virtual method. Had the invocation in B been written ((A)this).PrintFields(), it would recursively invoke the PrintFields method declared in B, not the one declared in A, since PrintFields is virtual and the run-time type of ((A)this) is B.

Only by including an override modifier can a method override another method. In all other cases, a method with the same signature as an inherited method simply hides the inherited method. In the example

```
class A
{
    public virtual void F() {}
}

class B: A
{
    public virtual void F() {}            // Warning, hiding inherited F()
}
```

the F method in B does not include an override modifier and therefore does not override the F method in A. Rather, the F method in B hides the method in A, and a warning is reported because the declaration does not include a new modifier.

In the example

```
class A
{
    public virtual void F() {}
}

class B: A
{
    new private void F() {}               // Hides A.F within B
}

class C: B
{
    public override void F() {}     // Ok, overrides A.F
}
```

the F method in B hides the virtual F method inherited from A. Since the new F in B has private access, its scope only includes the class body of B and does not extend to C. The declaration of F in C is therefore permitted to override the F inherited from A.

Sealed methods

When an instance method declaration includes a sealed modifier, the method is said to be a *sealed method*. A sealed method overrides an inherited virtual method with the same signature.

An override method can also be marked with the sealed modifier. Use of this modifier prevents a derived class from further overriding the method. The sealed modifier can only be used in combination with the override modifier.

The example

```
class A
{
    public virtual void F() {
            Console.WriteLine("A.F");
    }
    public virtual void G() {
            Console.WriteLine("A.G");
    }
}
```

```
class B: A
{
    sealed override public void F() {
        Console.WriteLine("B.F");
    }
    override public void G() {
        Console.WriteLine("B.G");
    }
}
class C: B
{
    override public void G() {
        Console.WriteLine("C.G");
    }
}
```

the class B provides two override methods: an F method that has the sealed modifier and a G method that does not. B's use of the sealed modifier prevents C from further overriding F.

Abstract methods

When an instance method declaration includes an abstract modifier, the method is said to be an *abstract method*. Although an abstract method is implicitly also a virtual method, it cannot have the virtual modifier.

An abstract method declaration introduces a new virtual method but does not provide an implementation of the method. Instead, non-abstract derived classes are required to provide their own implementation by overriding the method. Because an abstract method provides no actual implementation, the *method-body* of an abstract method simply consists of a semicolon.

Abstract method declarations are only permitted in abstract classes.

It is an error for an abstract method declaration to include the static or extern modifiers.

In the example

```
public abstract class Shape
{
    public abstract void Paint(Graphics g, Rectangle r);
}
public class Ellipse: Shape
{
    public override void Paint(Graphics g, Rectangle r) {
        g.drawEllipse(r);
    }
}
public class Box: Shape
{
    public override void Paint(Graphics g, Rectangle r) {
        g.drawRect(r);
    }
}
```

the Shape class defines the abstract notion of a geometrical shape object that can paint itself. The Paint method is abstract because there is no meaningful default implementation. The Ellipse and

Box classes are concrete Shape implementations. Because these classes are non-abstract, they are required to override the Paint method and provide an actual implementation.

It is an error for a *base-access* to reference an abstract method. In the example

```
class A
{
    public abstract void F();
}
class B: A
{
    public override void F() {
        base.F();                                  // Error, base.F is
    abstract
    }
}
```

an error is reported for the base.F() invocation because it references an abstract method.

An abstract method declaration is permitted to override a virtual method. This allows an abstract class to force re-implementation of the method in derived classes, and makes the original implementation of the method unavailable. In the example

```
class A
{
    public virtual void F() {
        Console.WriteLine("A.F");
    }
}
abstract class B: A
{
    public abstract override void F();
}
class C: B
{
    public override void F() {
        Console.WriteLine("C.F");
    }
}
```

class A declares a virtual method, class B overrides this method with an abstract method, and class C overrides the abstract method to provide its own implementation.

External methods

When a method declaration includes an extern modifier, the method is said to be an ***external method***. External methods are implemented externally, using a language other than C#. Because an external method declaration provides no actual implementation, the *method-body* of an external method simply consists of a semicolon.

The extern modifier is typically used in conjunction with a DllImport attribute, allowing external methods to be implemented by DLLs (Dynamic Link Libraries). The execution environment may support other mechanisms whereby implementations of external methods can be provided.

It is an error for an external method declaration to also include the abstract modifier. When an external method includes a DllImport attribute, the method declaration must also include a static modifier.

This example demonstrates the use of the extern modifier and the DllImport attribute:

```
class Path
{
    [DllImport("kernel32", setLastError=true)]
    static extern bool CreateDirectory(string name, SecurityAttributes sa);

    [DllImport("kernel32", setLastError=true)]
    static extern bool RemoveDirectory(string name);

    [DllImport("kernel32", setLastError=true)]
    static extern int GetCurrentDirectory(int bufSize, StringBuilder buf);

    [DllImport("kernel32", setLastError=true)]
    static extern bool SetCurrentDirectory(string name);
}
```

❖ Properties

In C#, properties are nothing but natural extension of data fields. They are usually known as 'smart fields' in C# community. We know that data encapsulation and hiding are the two fundamental characteristics of any object oriented programming language.In C#, data encapsulation is possible through either classes or structures. By using various access modifiers like private, public, protected, internal etc it is possible to control the accessibility of the class members.

Usually inside a class, we declare a data field as private and will provide a set of public SET and GET methods to access the data fields. This is a good programming practice, since the data fields are not directly accessible out side the class. We must use the set/get methods to access the data fields.

An example, which uses a set of set/get methods, is shown below.
```
        //SET/GET methods
        using System;
        class MyClass
        {
                private int x;
                public void SetX(int i)
                {
                        x = i;
                }
                public int GetX()
                {
                        return x;
                }
        }
        class MyClient
        {
                public static void Main()
                {
                        MyClass mc = new MyClass();
                        mc.SetX(10);
                        int xVal = mc.GetX();
                        Console.WriteLine(xVal);//Displays 10
                }
        }
```
But C# provides a built in mechanism called properties to do the above. In C#, properties are defined using the property declaration syntax. The general form of declaring a property is as follows.

```
<acces_modifier> <return_type> <property_name>
{
        get
        {
        }
        set
        {
        }
}
```

Where <access_modifier> can be private, public, protected or internal. The <return_type> can be any valid C# type. Note that the first part of the syntax looks quite similar to a field declaration and second part consists of a get accessor and a set accessor.

For example the above program can be modifies with a property X as follows.

```
class MyClass
{
        private int x;
        public int X
        {
                get
                {
                        return x;
                }
                set
                {
                x = value;
                }
        }
}
```

The object of the class MyClass can access the property X as follows.

MyClass mc = new MyClass();

mc.X = 10; // calls set accessor of the property X, and pass 10 as value of the standard field 'value'. This is used for setting value for the data member x.

Console.WriteLine(mc.X);// displays 10. Calls the get accessor of the property X.

The complete program is shown below.

```
using System;
class MyClass
{
        private int x;
        public int X
        {
                get
                {
                        return x;
                }
                set
                {
                        x = value;
                }
```

```
        }
}
class MyClient
{
        public static void Main()
        {
                MyClass mc = new MyClass();
                mc.X = 10;
                int xVal = mc.X;
                Console.WriteLine(xVal);//Displays 10
        }
}
```

Remember that a property should have at least one accessor, either set or get. The set accessor has a free variable available in it called value, which gets created automatically by the compiler. We can't declare any variable with the name value inside the set accessor.

We can do very complicated calculations inside the set or get accessor. Even they can throw exceptions.

Since normal data fields and properties are stored in the same memory space, in C#, it is not possible to declare a field and property with the same name.

Static Properties

C# also supports static properties, which belongs to the class rather than to the objects of the class. All the rules applicable to a static member are applicable to static properties also.

The following program shows a class with a static property.

```
using System;
class MyClass
{
        private static int x;
        public static int X
        {
                get
                {
                        return x;
                }
                set
                {
                        x = value;
                }
        }
}
class MyClient
{
        public static void Main()
        {
                MyClass.X = 10;
                int xVal = MyClass.X;
                Console.WriteLine(xVal);//Displays 10
        }
}
```

Remember that set/get accessor of static property can access only other static members of the class. Also static properties are invoking by using the class name.

Properties & Inheritance

The properties of a Base class can be inherited to a Derived class.

```
using System;
class Base
{
        public int X
        {
                get{Console.Write("Base GET");return 10;}
                set{Console.Write("Base SET");}
        }
}
class Derived : Base
{
        class MyClient
        {
                public static void Main()
                {
                        Derived d1 = new Derived();
                        d1.X = 10;
                        Console.WriteLine(d1.X);//Displays 'Base SET Base GET 10'
                }
        }
}
```

The above program is very straightforward. The inheritance of properties is just like inheritance any other member.

Properties & Polymorphism

A Base class property can be polymorphicaly overridden in a Derived class. But remember that the modifiers like virtual, override etc are using at property level, not at accessor level.

```
using System;
class Base
{
        public virtual int X
        {
                get
                {
                        Console.Write("Base GET");
                        return 10;
                }
                set
                {
                        Console.Write("Base SET");
                }
        }
}
class Derived : Base
{
```

```
        public override int X
        {
                get
                {
                        Console.Write("Derived GET");
                        return 10;
                }
                set
                {
                        Console.Write("Derived SET");
                }
        }
}
class MyClient
{
        public static void Main()
        {
                Base b1 = new Derived();
                b1.X = 10;
                Console.WriteLine(b1.X);//Displays 'Derived SET Derived GET 10'
        }
}
```

Abstract Properties

A property inside a class can be declared as abstract by using the keyword abstract. Remember that an abstract property in a class carries no code at all. The get/set accessors are simply represented with a semicolon. In the derived class we must implement both set and get assessors.

If the abstract class contains only set accessor, we can implement only set in the derived class.

The following program shows an abstract property in action.

```
using System;
abstract class Abstract
{
        public abstract int X
        {
                get;
                set;
        }
}
class Concrete : Abstract
{
        public override int X
        {
                get
                {
                        Console.Write(" GET");
                        return 10;
                }
                set
                {
                        Console.Write(" SET");
                }
```

```
        }
}
class MyClient
{
        public static void Main()
        {
                Concrete c1 = new Concrete();
                c1.X = 10;
                Console.WriteLine(c1.X);//Displays 'SET GET 10'
        }
}
```

The properties are an important features added in language level inside C#. They are very useful in GUI🔍 programming. Remember that the compiler actually generates the appropriate getter and setter methods when it parses the C# property syntax.

❖ Indexer

C# introduces a new concept known as Indexerswhich are used for treating an object as an array. The indexers areusually known as smart arrays in C# community. Defining a C# indexer ismuch like defining properties. We can say that an indexer is a memberthat enables an object to be indexed in the same way as an array.

```
<modifier> <return type> this [argument list]{
        get
        {
                // Get codes goes here
        }

        set
        {
                // Set codes goes here
        }
}
```

Where the modifier can be private, public, protected or internal. The return type can be any valid C# types. The 'this' is a special keyword in C# to indicate the object of the current class. The formal-argument-list specifies the parameters of the indexer. The formal parameter list of an indexer corresponds to that of a method, except that at least one parameter must be specified, and that the ref and out parameter modifiers are not permitted. Remember that indexers in C# must have at least one parameter. Otherwise the compiler will generate a compilation error.

The following program shows a C# indexer in action

```
using System;
using System.Collections;
class MyClass
```

```
{
        private string []data = new string[5];
        public string this [int index]
        {
                get
                {
                        return data[index];
                }
                set
                {
                        data[index] = value;
                }
        }
}
class MyClient
{
        public static void Main()
        {
                MyClass mc = new MyClass();
                mc[0] = "Rajesh";
                mc[1] = "A3-126";
                mc[2] = "Snehadara";
                mc[3] = "Irla";
                mc[4] = "Mumbai";
                Console.WriteLine("{0},{1},{2},{3},{4}",mc[0],mc[1],mc[2],mc[3],mc[4]);
        }
}
```

The indexers in C# can be overloaded just like member functions. The formal parameter list of an indexer defines the signature of the indexer. Specifically, the signature of an indexer consists of the number and types of its formal parameters. The element type is not part of an indexer's signature, nor is the names of the formal parameters. The signature of an indexer must differ from the signatures of all other indexers declared in the same class. C# do not have the concept of static indexers. If we declare an indexer static, the compiler will show a compilation time error.

Indexers & Inheritance

Just like any other class members, indexers can also participate in inheritance. A base class indexer is inherited to the derived class.

```
using System;
class Base
{
        public int this[int indxer]
        {
```

```
        Get
        {
                Console.Write("Base GET");
                return 10;
        }
        Set
        {
                Console.Write("Base SET");
        }
    }
}
class Derived : Base
{
}
class MyClient
{
        public static void Main()
        {
                Derived d1 = new Derived();
                d1[0] = 10;
                Console.WriteLine(d1[0]);//Displays 'Base SET Base GET 10'
        }
}
```

Indexers & Polymorphism

A Base class indexer can be polymorphicalyoverridden in a Derived class. But remember that the modifiers likevirtual, override etc are using at property level, not at accessorlevel.

```
using System;
class Base
{
        public virtual int this[int index]
        {
                get
                {
                        Console.Write("Base GET");
                        return 10;
                }
                set
                {
                        Console.Write("Base SET");
                }
        }
}
class Derived : Base
```

```
{
        public override int this[int index]
        {
                get
                {
                        Console.Write("Derived GET");
                        return 10;
                }
                set
                {
                        Console.Write("Derived SET");
                }
        }
}
class MyClient
{
        public static void Main()
        {
                Base b1 = new Derived();
                b1[0]= 10;
                Console.WriteLine(b1[0]);//Displays 'Derived SET Derived GET 10'
        }
}
```

Abstract Indexers

An indexer inside a class can be declared asabstract by using the keyword abstract. Remember that an abstractindexer in a class carries no code at all. The get/set accessors aresimply represented with a semicolon. In the derived class we mustimplement both set and get assessors.

If the abstract class contains only set accessor, we can implement only set in the derived class.

The following program shows an abstract indexer in action.

```
using System;
abstract class Abstract
{
        public abstract int this[int index]
        {
                get;
                set;
        }
}
class Concrete : Abstract
{
```

```csharp
        public override int this[int index]
        {
                Get                     .
                {
                        Console.Write(" GET");
                        return 10;
                }
                Set
                {
                        Console.Write(" SET");
                }
        }
}
class MyClient
{
        public static void Main()
        {
                Concrete c1 = new Concrete();
                c1[0] = 10;
                Console.WriteLine(c1[0]);//Displays 'SET GET 10'
        }
}
```

Indexers & Properties

1. An index is identified by it's signature. But a property is identified it's name.
2. An indexer is always an instance member, but a property can be static also.
3. An indexer is accessed through an element access. But a property is through a member access.

Chapter 3: Inheritance

❖ Inheritance

Inheritance is a way to compartmentalize and reuse code by creating collections of attributes and behaviors called objects which can be based on previously created objects. In *classical inheritance* where objects are defined by classes, classes can inherit other classes. The new classes, known as **Sub-classes** (or derived classes), inherit attributes and behavior of the pre-existing classes, which are referred to as **Super-classes** (or ancestor classes). The inheritance relationship of sub- and superclasses gives rise to a hierarchy. In Prototype-based programming objects can be defined directly from other objects without the need to define any classes.

C# supports two types of Inheritance mechanisms

1) Implementation Inheritance
2) Interface Inheritance

Implementation inheritance means that a type derives from a base type, taking all the base type's member fields and functions. With implementation inheritance, a derived type adopts the base type's implementation of each function, unless it is indicated in the definition of the derived type that a function implementation is to be overridden. This type of inheritance is most useful when you need to add functionality to an existing type, or when a number of related types share a significant amount of common functionality.

Interface inheritance means that a type inherits only the signatures of the functions and does not inherit any implementations. This type of inheritance is most useful when you want to spec-ify that a type makes certain features available. For example, certain types can indicate that they provide a resource cleanup method called Dispose() by deriving from an interface, System.IDisposable. Because the way that one type cleans up resources is likely to be very different from the way that another type cleans up resources, there is no point in defining any common implementation, so interface inheritance is appropriate here. Interface inheritance is often regarded as providing a contract: By deriving from an interface, a type is guaranteed to provide certain functionality to clients.

➢ Method Overload

C# allows you to define different versions of a method in class, and the compiler will automatically select the most appropriate one based on the parameters supplied.

Declearing Oparetor overloading

While display a integer we can write:

```
int x = 10;
Console.WriteLine (x);
```

While display a integer we can write:

```
string Message = "Hello";
Console.WriteLine (Message);
```

How is this possible? what parameter type does Console.WriteLine () take? If it was expecting to take a string, then the first of these two examples would give error, because there is no implicit cast from int to string.

If Console.WriteLine () was expecting to take any numaric dat type however, then the second of these examples would give a compilation error there is no implicit cast from string to any numaric type. Yet fact, both of these lines will compile without error and run to give the expected results.

The reason is that there are two diffrent Console.writeLine( ) methods - one of them takes an int as parameter, the other one takes a string.

add Method Overloading?

In addition of two or three integers, we add two integer values as a method, add three integer values as a method, as well. i.e:

```
public class AddingNumbers
{
    public int Add(int a, int b)
    {
        return a+b;
    }

    public int Add(int a, int b, int c)
    {
        return a+b+c;
    }

}
```

Calling Overloaded Methods?

```
public int add(int x, int y)
public int add(int x, int y, int z)
```

We've also assumed that two overloaded methods.

Overload 1 requires two integers - exactly the parameters that we are passing in. The compiler will generate code that calls this overload.

Overload 2 requires three integers.

When to use Method Overloading?

Generally, you should consider overloading a method when you for some reason need a couple of methods that take different perameters, but conceptually do the same thing. Console.WriteLine( ) is a good example. Another good example method is a method

Sign( ) in the System.Math base class, which returns the sign of a number, and is overloaded to work out the sign of double, a decimal and other signed types.

In general, you should not use overloads when two methods really do diffrent things - otherwise you'll simply confuse the developers who have to use your classes.

All unary and binary operators have pre-defined implementations, that are automatically available in any expressions. In addition to this pre-defined implementations, user defined implementations can also be introduced in C#. The mechanism of giving a special meaning to a standard C# operator with respect to a user defined data type such as classes or structures is known as operator overloading. Remember that it is not possible to overload all operators in C#. The following table shows the operators and their overloadability in C#.

➢ **Operator Overload**

+, -, *, /, %, &, |, <<, >> All C# binary operators can be overloaded.

+, -, !, ~, ++, −, true, false All C# unary operators can be overloaded.

==, !=, <, >, <= , >= All relational operators can be overloaded, but only as pairs.

&&, || They can't be overloaded

() (Conversion operator) They can't be overloaded

+=, -=, *=, /=, %= These compound assignment operators can be overloaded. But in C#, these operators are automatically overloaded when the respective binary operator is overloaded.

=, . , ?:, ->, new, is, as, size of These operators can't be overloaded

In C#, a special function called operator function is used for overloading purpose. These special function or method must be public and static. They can take only value arguments.The ref and out parameters are not allowed as arguments to operator functions. The general form of an operator function is as follows.

public static return_type operator op (argument list)

Where the op is the operator to be overloaded and operator is the required keyword. For overloading the unary operators, there is only one argument and for overloading a binary operator there are two arguments. Remember that at least one of the arguments must be a user-defined type such as class or struct type.

Overloading Unary Operators – the general form of operator function for unary operators is as follows.public static return_type operator op (Type t){// Statements}Where Type must be a class or struct.the return type can be any type except void for unary operators like +,~, ! and dot (.). but the return type must be the type of 'Type' for ++and o remember that the true and false operators can be overloaded only as pairs. The compilation error occurs if a class declares one of these operators without declaring the other.

The following program overloads the unary – operator inside the class Complex

```
using System;
class Complex
{
        private int x;
        private int y;
        public Complex()
        {
        }
        public Complex(int i, int j)
        {
                x = i;
                y = j;
        }
        public void ShowXY()
        {
                Console.WriteLine(\"{0} {1}\",x,y);
        }
        public static Complex operator -(Complex c)
        {
                Complex temp = new Complex();
                temp.x = -c.x;
                temp.y = -c.y;
                return temp;
        }
}
class MyClient
{
        public static void Main()
        {
                Complex c1 = new Complex(10,20);
                c1.ShowXY(); // displays 10 & 20
                Complex c2 = new Complex();
                c2.ShowXY(); // displays 0 & 0
                c2 = -c1;
                c2.ShowXY(); // diapls -10 & -20
        }
}
```

C# Programming Made Easy

Overloading Binary Operators

An overloaded binary operator must take two arguments, at least one of them must be of the type class or struct, inwhich the operation is defined. But overloaded binary operators can return any value except the type void. The general form of a overloaded binary operator is as follows.

```
public static return_type operator op (Type1 t1, Type2 t2)
{
//Statements
}
```

A concrete example is given below

```
using System;
class Complex
{
        private int x;
        private int y;
        public Complex()
        {
        }
        public Complex(int i, int j)
        {
                x = i;
                y = j;
        }
        public void ShowXY()
        {
                Console.WriteLine(\"{0} {1}\",x,y);
        }
        public static Complex operator +(Complex c1,Complex c2)
        {
                Complex temp = new Complex();
                temp.x = c1.x+c2.x;
                temp.y = c1.y+c2.y;
                return temp;
        }
}
class MyClient
{
        public static void Main()
        {
                Complex c1 = new Complex(10,20);
                c1.ShowXY(); // displays 10 & 20
                Complex c2 = new Complex(20,30);
```

```
        c2.ShowXY(); // displays 20 & 30
        Complex c3 = new Complex();
        c3 = c1 + c2;
        c3.ShowXY(); // dislplays 30 & 50
    }
}
```

The binary operators such as = =, ! =, <,>, < =, > = can be overloaded only as pairs. Remember that when a binary arithmetic operator is overloaded, corresponding assignment operators also get overloaded automatically. For example if we overload + operator, it implicitly overloads the + = operator also.

❖ Interface

To rectify the drawback of multiple inheritance, the creators of C# have introduced a new concept called interfaces. Java programmers may be well aware of this concept. All interfaces should be declared with the keyword *interface*. You can implement any number of interfaces in a single derived class, but you should provide signatures to all method definitions of the corresponding interfaces. To illustrate, Listing 1 shows how to declare interfaces and implement them in a class:

```
using System;

interface Interdemo
{
 void Show();
}

class Interimp:Interdemo
{
 public void Show()
 {
  Console.WriteLine("Show() method Implemented");
 }

 public static void Main(string[] args)
 {
  Interimp inter = new Interimp();
  inter.Show();
 }
}
```

Combining Interfaces

Two or more interfaces can be combined into a single interface and implemented in a class.

```
using System;
interface Interdemo
{
 void Show();
}

interface Interdemo1
```

```
{
  void Display();
}

interface Combineinter:Interdemo,Interdemo1
{
  //Above interfaces combined
}

class Multipleinterimp:Combineinter
{
  public void Show()
  {
    Console.WriteLine("Show() method Implemented");
  }

  public void Display()
  {
    Console.WriteLine("Display() method Implemented");
  }

  public static void Main(string[] args)
  {
    Multipleinterimp inter = new Multipleinterimp();
    inter.Show();
    inter.Display();
  }
}
```

You easily can determine whether a particular interface is implemented in a class by using is and as operators. The *is* operator enables you to check whether one type or class is compatible with another type or class; it returns a Boolean value. Listing 3 illustrates the usage of the *is* operator by revisiting Listing 2.

```
using System;

interface Interdemo
{
  bool Show();
}

interface Interdemo1
{
  bool Display();
}

class Interimp:Interdemo
{
  public bool Show()
  {
    Console.WriteLine("Show() method Implemented");
    return true;
  }

  public static void Main(string[] args)
```

```
{
  Interimp inter = new Interimp();
  inter.Show();

  if(inter is Interdemo1)
  {
    Interdemo1 id = (Interdemo1)inter;
    bool ok = id.Display();
    Console.WriteLine("Method Implemented");
  }

  else
  {
    Console.WriteLine("Method not implemented");
  }
 }
}
```

Whereas the *is* operator returns a boolean value as shown in the preceding listing, the *as* operator returns null if there is any incompatibility between types. Listing 4 examines the usage of this operator. Here we have revisited Listing 3. Notice the change in code inside the Main () method.

```
using System;

interface Interdemo
{
  bool Show();
}

interface Interdemo1
{
  bool Display();
}

class Interimpas:Interdemo
{
  public bool Show()
  {
    Console.WriteLine("Show() method Implemented");
    return true;
  }

  public static void Main(string[] args)
  {
    Interimpas inter = new Interimpas();
    inter.Show();

    Interdemo1 id = inter as Interdemo1;

    if(null!=id)
    {

      bool ok = id.Display();
      Console.WriteLine("Method Implemented");
    }
```

```
  else
  {
    Console.WriteLine("Method not implemented");
   }
 }
}
```

Avoiding Name Ambiguity

Suppose you are declaring same method definitions in two different interfaces. The compiler will naturally show an error due to the ambiguity of the implemented method. Even if you use the "is" keyword, the compiler still will show warnings. To avoid this, you have to follow the syntax as shown in Listing 5

```
using System;

interface Interdemo
{
  void Show();
}

interface Interdemo1
{
  void Show();
}


class Interclash:Interdemo,Interdemo1
{
  void Interdemo.Show()
  {
    Console.WriteLine("Show() method Implemented");
  }

  void Interdemo1.Show()
  {
    Console.WriteLine("Display() method Implemented");
  }

  public static void Main(string[] args)
  {
    Interclash inter = new Interclash();
    inter.Interdemo.Show();
    inter.Interdemo1.Show();
  }
}
```

Chapter 4: Pointers and Delegate

❖ Pointers

C# also supports pointers in a limited extent. A pointer is nothing but a variable that holds the memory address of another type. But in C# pointer can only be declared to hold the memory address of value types and arrays. Unlike reference types, pointer types are not tracked by the default garbage collection mechanism. For the same reason pointers are not allowed to point to a reference type or even to a structure type which contains a reference type. We can say that pointers can point to only unmanaged types which includes all basic data types, enum types, other pointer types and structs which contain only unmanaged types.

➤ Declaring a Pointer type

The general form of declaring a pointer type is as shown below

type *variable_name;

Where * is known as the de-reference operator. For example the following statement

int *x ;

Declares a pointer variable x, which can hold the address of an int type. The reference operator (&) can be used to get the memory address of a variable.

int x = 100;

The &x gives the memory address of the variable x, which we can assign to a pointer variable

int *ptr = & x;.
Console.WriteLine((int)ptr) // Displays the memory address
Console.WriteLine(*ptr) // Displays the value at the memory address.

➤ Unsafe Codes

The C# statements can be executed either as in a safe or in an unsafe context. The statements marked as unsafe by using the keyword unsafe runs out side the control of Garbage Collector. Remember that in C# any code involving pointers requires an unsafe context.

We can use the unsafe keyword in two different ways. It can be used as a modifier to a method, property, and constructor etc. For example

```csharp
using System;
class MyClass
{
        public unsafe void Method()
        {
                int x = 10;
                int y = 20;
                int *ptr1 = &x;
                int *ptr2 = &y;
                Console.WriteLine((int)ptr1);
                Console.WriteLine((int)ptr2);
                Console.WriteLine(*ptr1);
                Console.WriteLine(*ptr2);
        }
}
class MyClient
{
        public static void Main()
        {
                MyClass mc = new MyClass();
                mc.Method();
        }
}
```

The keyword unsafe can also be used to mark a group of statements as unsafe as shown below.

```csharp
//unsafe blocks
using System;
class MyClass
{
        public void Method()
        {
                unsafe
                {
                        int x = 10;
                        int y = 20;
                        int *ptr1 = &x;
                        int *ptr2 = &y;
                        Console.WriteLine((int)ptr1);
                        Console.WriteLine((int)ptr2);
                        Console.WriteLine(*ptr1);
                        Console.WriteLine(*ptr2);
                }
        }
```

```
        }

class MyClient
{
        public static void Main()
        {
                MyClass mc = new MyClass();
                mc.Method();
        }
}
```

➢ **Pinning an Object**

The C# garbage collector can move the objects in memory as it wishes during the garbage collection process. The C# provides a special keyword fixed to tell Garbage Collector not to move an object. That means this fixes in memory the location of the value types pointed to. This is what is known as pinning in C#.

The fixed statement is typically implemented by generating tables that describe to the Garbage Collector, which objects are to remain fixed in which regions of executable code. Thus as long as a Garbage Collector process doesn't actually occur during execution of fixed statements, there is very little cost associated with this. However when a Garbage Collector process does occur, fixed objects may cause fragmentation of the heap. Hence objects should be fixed only when absolutely necessary and only for the shortest amount of time.

➢ **Pointers & Methods**

The points can be passed as argument to a method as showing below. The methods can also return a pointer.

```
using System;
class MyClass
{
        public unsafe void Method()
        {
                int x = 10;
                int y = 20;
                int *sum = swap(&x,&y);
                Console.WriteLine(*sum);
        }
        public unsafe int* swap(int *x, int *y)
        {
                int sum;
                sum = *x + *y;
```

```
            return &sum;
        }
    }
    class MyClient
    {
        public static void Main()
        {
            MyClass mc = new MyClass();
            mc.Method();
        }
    }
```

➢ Pointers & Conversions

In C# pointer types do not inherit from object and no conversion exists between pointer types and objects. That means boxing and un-boxing are not supported by pointers. But C# supports conversions between the different pointer types and pointer types and integral types.

C# supports both implicit and explicit pointer conversions within un-safe context. The implicit conversions are

1. From any type pointer type to void * type.
2. From null type to any pointer type.

The cast operator (()) is necessary for any explicit type conversions. The explicit type conversions are

1. From any pointer type to any other pointer type.
2. From sbyte, byte, short, ushort, int, uint, long, ulong to any pointer type.
3. From any pointer type to sbyte, byte, short, ushort, int, uint, long, ulong types.

For example

```
char c = 'R';
char *pc = &c;
void *pv = pc; // Implicit conversion
int *pi = (int *) pv; // Explicit conversion using casting operator
```

➢ Pointers & Arrays

In C# array elements can be accessed by using pointer notations.

```
using System;
class MyClass
{
```

```
public unsafe void Method()
{
        int []iArray = new int[10];
        for(int count=0; count < 10; count++)
        {
                iArray[count] = count*count;
        }
        fixed(int *ptr = iArray)
        Display(ptr);
        //Console.WriteLine(*(ptr+2));
        //Console.WriteLine((int)ptr);
}
public unsafe void Display(int *pt)
{
        for(int i=0; i < 14;i++)
        {
                Console.WriteLine(*(pt+i));
        }
}
}
class MyClient
{
        public static void Main()
        {
                MyClass mc = new MyClass();
                mc.Method();
        }
}
```

> **Pointers & Structures**

The structures in C# are value types. The pointers can be used with structures if it contains only value types as its members. For example

```
using System;
struct MyStruct
{
        public int x;
        public int y;
        public void SetXY(int i, int j)
        {
                x = i;
                y = j;
        }
        public void ShowXY()
        {
```

```
        Console.WriteLine(x);
        Console.WriteLine(y);
    }
}

class MyClient
{
    public unsafe static void Main()
    {
        MyStruct ms = new MyStruct();
        MyStruct *ms1 = &ms;
        ms1->SetXY(10,20);
        ms1->ShowXY();
    }
}
```

❖ Delegates

A delegate is a type that references a method. Once a delegate is assigned a method, it behaves exactly like that method. The delegate method can be used like any other method, with parameters and a return value, as in this example:

public delegate type_of_delegate delegate_name(arguments);

Example:

public delegate int mydelegate(int delvar1,int delvar2)

Any method that matches the delegate's signature, which consists of the return type and parameters, can be assigned to the delegate. This makes is possible to programmatically change method calls, and also plug new code into existing classes. As long as you know the delegate's signature, you can assign your own delegated method.

This ability to refer to a method as a parameter makes delegates ideal for defining callback methods. For example, a sort algorithm could be passed a reference to the method that compares two objects. Separating the comparison code allows the algorithm to be written in a more general way.

Delegates have the following properties:

- Delegates are similar to C++ function pointers, but are type safe.
- Delegates allow methods to be passed as parameters.
- Delegates can be used to define callback methods.
- Delegates can be chained together
- Methods don't need to match the delegate signature exactly.

Where are Delegates used?

Events

The most common example of using delegates is in events. You define a method that contains code for performing various tasks when an event (such as a mouse click) takes place. This method needs to be invoked by the runtime when the event occurs. Hence this method, that you defined, is passed as a parameter to a delegate.

Threads / Parallel Processing

You defined several methods and you wish to execute them simultaneously and in parallel to whatever else the application is doing. This can be achieved by starting new threads. To start a new thread for your method you pass your method details to a delegate.

Generic Classes

Delegates are also used for generic class libraries which have generic functionality defined. However the generic class may need to call certainfunctions defined by the end user implementing the generic class. This can be done by passing the user defined functions to delegates.

Sample Program using Delegate

```
public delegate double Delegate_Prod(int a,int b);
class Class1
{
    static double fn_Prodvalues(int val1,int val2)
    {
        return val1*val2;
    }
    static void Main(string[] args)
    {
        //Creating the Delegate Instance
        Delegate_Prod delObj = new Delegate_Prod(fn_Prodvalues);
        Console.Write("Please Enter Values");
        int v1 = Int32.Parse(Console.ReadLine());
        int v2 = Int32.Parse(Console.ReadLine());
        //use a delegate for processing
        double res = delObj(v1,v2);
        Console.WriteLine ("Result :"+res);
        Console.ReadLine();
    }
}
```

> **Multicast Delegates**

Delegate's ability to multicast means that a delegate object can maintain a list of methods to call, rather than a single method if you want to add a method to the invocation list of a delegate object , you simply make use of the overloaded += operator, and if you want to remove a method from the invocation list you make use of the overloaded operator -= .

The Multicast delegate here contain methods that return void, if you want to create a multicast delegate with return type you will get the return type of the last method in the invocation list.

Simple Program using Multicast Delegate

```
delegate void Delegate_Multicast(int x, int y);
Class Class2
{
    static void Method1(int x, int y)
    {
        Console.WriteLine("You r in Method 1");
    }

    static void Method2(int x, int y)
    {
        Console.WriteLine("You r in Method 2");
    }

    public static void "on" />Main()
    {
        Delegate_Multicast func = new Delegate_Multicast(Method1);
        func += new Delegate_Multicast(Method2);
        func(1,2);        // Method1 and Method2 are called
        func -= new Delegate_Multicast(Method1);
        func(2,3);        // Only Method2 is called
    }
}
```

> **Anonymous Methods**

Up to this point, a method must already exist in order for the delegate to work (that is, the delegate is defined with the same signature as the method(s) it will be used with). However, there is another way to use delegates — with anonymous methods. An anonymous method is a block of code that is used as the parameter for the delegate.

The syntax for defining a delegate with an anonymous method doesn ' t change. It ' s when the delegate is instantiated that things change. The following is a very simple console application that shows how using an anonymous method can work:
using System;

```
namespace Wrox.ProCSharp.Delegates
{
        class Program
        {
                delegate string DelegateTest(string val);
                static void Main()
                {
                        string mid = ", middle part,";
                        DelegateTest anonDel = delegate(string param)
                        {
                                param += mid;
                                param += " and this was added to the string.";
                                return param;
                        };
                        Console.WriteLine(anonDel("Start of string"));
                }
        }
}
```

The delegate DelegateTest is defined inside the class Program . It takes a single string parameter. Where things become different is in the Main method. When anonDel is defined, instead of passing in a known method name, a simple block of code is used, prefixed by the delegate keyword, followed by a parameter:

```
delegate (string param)
{
        param += mid;
        param += " and this was added to the string.";
        return param;
};
```

As you can see, the block of code uses a method - level string variable, mid , which is defined outside of the anonymous method and adds it to the parameter that was passed in. The code then returns the string value. When the delegate is called, a string is passed in as the parameter and the returned string is output to the console.

The benefit of anonymous methods is to reduce the code you have to write. You don't have to define a method just to use it with a delegate. This becomes very evident when defining the delegate for an event. (Events are discussed later in this chapter.) This can help reduce the complexity of code, especially where there are several events defined. With anonymous methods, the code does not perform faster. The compiler still defines a method; the method just has an automatically assigned name that you don't need to know.

A couple of rules must be followed when using anonymous methods. You can't have a jump statement (break , goto , or continue) in an anonymous method that has a target outside of

C# Programming Made Easy

the anonymous method. The reverse is also true — a jump statement outside the anonymous method cannot have a target inside the anonymous method. Unsafe code cannot be accessed inside an anonymous method. Also, ref and out parameters that are used outside of the anonymous method cannot be accessed. Other variables defined outside of the anonymous method can be used.

If you have to write the same functionality more than once, don't use anonymous methods. In this case, instead of duplicating the code, writing a named method is the preferred way. You only have to write it once and reference it by its name.

❖ Events

The Event model in C# finds its roots in the event programming model that is popular in asynchronous programming. The basic foundation behind this programming model is the idea of "publisher and subscribers." In this model, you have publishers who will do some logic and publish an "event." Publishers will then send out their event only to subscribers who have subscribed to receive the specific event.

In C#, any object can publish a set of events to which other applications can subscribe. When the publishing class raises an event, all the subscribed applications are notified. The following figure shows this mechanism.

The following important conventions are used with events:

- Event Handlers in the .NET Framework return void and take two parameters.
- The first paramter is the source of the event; that is the publishing object.
- The second parameter is an object derived from EventArgs.
- Events are properties of the class publishing the event.
- The keyword event controls how the event property is accessed by the subscribing classes.

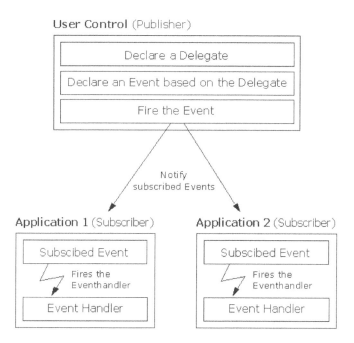

> ➤ **Declaring Events**

Declaring an event is directly tied to a delegate. A delegate object encapsulates a method so that it can be called anonymously. An event is a mechanism by which a client class can pass in delegates to methods that need to be invoked whenever "something happens". When it does, the delegate(s) given to it by its clients are invoked.

To declare an event in C# use the following syntax:

```
public delegate void testDelegate(int a);
public event testDelegate MyEvent;
```

Once an event is declared, it must be associated with one or more event handlers before it can be raised. An event handler is nothing but a method that is called using a delegate. Use the += operator to associate an event with an instance of a delegate that already exists.

For example:

```
Myform.MyEvent += new testEvent(MyMethod);
```

An event handler may also be detached as follows:

MyForm.MyEvent -= new testEvent(MyMethod);

In C#, events may be raised by just calling them by a name similar to method invocation, say MyEvent(10). The example given in the next section will help you understand events better.

➤ **How does the event keyword work ?**

Whenever an event is defined for a class, the compiler generates three methods that are used to manage the underlying delegate i.e.:

- add_<EventName>: This is a public method that calls the static Combine method of System.Delegate in order to add another method to its internal invocation list. This method is however not used explicitly. The same effect is achieved by using the += operator as specified before.

- remove_<EventName>: This is also a public method that calls the static Remove method of System.Delegate in order to remove a receiver from the event's invocation list. This method is also not called directly. Its job is done by the -= operator.

- raise_<EventName>: A protected method that calls the compiler generated Invoke method of the delegate, in order to call each method in the invocation list.

➤ **Event Creation**

An event is declared like a pseudo-variable but based on a delegate. Therefore, to declare an event, you must have a delegate that would implement it. Here is an example:

```
using System;

delegate void dlgSimple();

class Exercise
{
        public static void Welcome()
        {
        Console.WriteLine("Welcome to the Wonderful World of C# Programming!");
        }
}
```

To actually declare an event, you use the event keyword with the following formula:

[attributes] [modifiers] event type declarator;
[attributes] [modifiers] event type member-name {accessor-declarations};

The attributes factor can be a normal C# attribute.

The modifier can be one or a combination of the following keywords: **public, private, protected, internal, abstract, new, override, static, virtual, or extern.**

The event keyword is required. It is followed by the name of the delegate that specifies its behavior. If the event is declared in the main class, it should be made static. Like everything in a program, an event must have a name. This would allow the clients to know what (particular) event occurred. Here is an example:

```
using System;

delegate void dlgSimple();

class Exercise
{
    public static event dlgSimple Simply;

    public static void Welcome()
    {
        Console.WriteLine("Welcome to the Wonderful World of C# Programming!");
    }
}
```

After declaring the event, you must define a method that calls the event. Here is an example:

```
using System;

delegate void dlgSimple();

class Exercise
{
    public static event dlgSimple Simply;

    public static void Welcome()
    {
    Console.WriteLine("Welcome to the Wonderful World of C# Programming!");
    }

    public static void SayHello()
    {
        Simply();
    }
}
```

When the event occurs, its delegate would be invoked. This specification is also referred to as hooking up an event. As the event occurs (or fires), the method that implements the delegate runs. This provides complete functionality for the event and makes the event ready to be used. Before using an event, you must combine it to the method that implements it. This can be done by passing the name of the method to the appropriate delegate, as we learned when studying delegates. You can then assign this variable to the event's name using the += operator. Once this is done, you can call the event. Here is an example:

```
using System;
delegate void dlgSimple();
class Exercise
{
        public static event dlgSimple Simply;

        public static void Welcome()
        {
                Console.WriteLine("Welcome to the Wonderful World of C# Programming!");
        }

        public static void SayHello()
        {
                Simply();
        }

        static int Main()
        {
                Simply += new dlgSimple(Welcome);
                SayHello();
                return 0;
        }
}
```

Instead of the += operator used when initializing the event, you can implement add and remove of the event class. Here is an example:

```
using System;
delegate void dlgSimple();
class Exercise
{
    public event dlgSimple Simply
    {
        add
        {
                Simply += new dlgSimple(Welcome);
        }
        remove
        {
                Simply -= new dlgSimple(Welcome);
        }
    }
    public void Welcome()
    {
        Console.WriteLine("Welcome to the Wonderful World of C# Programming!");
    }
}
```

➢ **Event Implementation & Receiving**

To help understand how events are implemented and received, let's look at the traditional "Clock Timer" example. The Clock Timer generates an event each second and notifies the interested clients through events. First we define a public delegate for the event, calling it 'TimerEvent':

C# Programming Made Easy

public delegate void TimerEvent(object sender, EventArgs e);

Now we define a class named 'ClockTimer' to generate the event.

```
class ClockTimer
{
  public event TimerEvent Timer;
  public void Start()
  {
      for(int i=0; i<5; i++)
      {
        Timer(this, null);
        Thread.Sleep(1000);
      }
  }
}
```

The class contains an event, 'Timer', of type TimerEvent delegate. In the Start() method, the event 'Timer' is raised each second for a total of 5 times. Here, we have used the Sleep() method of the System.Threading.Thread class, which takes the number of milliseconds the current thread will be suspended as its argument. We will explore threading and its issues in coming lessons.

Next we need to define a class that will receive and consume the event, which is defined as:

```
class Test
{
  static void Main()
  {
    ClockTimer clockTimer = new ClockTimer();
      clockTimer.Timer += new TimerEvent(OnClockTick);
      clockTimer.Start();
  }
  public static void OnClockTick(object sender, EventArgs e)
  {
    Console.WriteLine("Received a clock tick event!");
  }
}
```

The class contains an event handler method, 'OnClockTick()', which follows the ClockEvent delegate's signature. In the Main() method of the class, we have created an instance of the event generator class 'ClockTimer'. Later we registered (or subscribed) the OnClockTick() event handler to the 'Timer' event of the ClockTimer class. Finally, we have called the Start() method, which will start the process of generating events in the ClockTimer class. The complete source code of the program is shown below.

```
using System;
using System.Threading;
namespace CSharpSchool
{
  class Test
  {
    static void Main()
    {
    ClockTimer clockTimer = new ClockTimer();
      clockTimer.Timer += new TimerEvent(OnClockTick);
      clockTimer.Start();
```

```
        }
        public static void OnClockTick(object sender, EventArgs e)
        {
        Console.WriteLine("Received a clock tick event!");
        }
}
public delegate void TimerEvent(object sender, EventArgs e);

class ClockTimer
{
        public event TimerEvent Timer;
        public void Start()
        {
          for(int i=0; i<5; i++)
          {
                Timer(this, null);
                Thread.Sleep(1000);
          }
        }
}
}
```

Note that we have also included the System.Threading namespace at the start of the program, as we are using its Thread class in our code. The output of the program is:

Received a clock tick event!
Received a clock tick event!
Received a clock tick event!
Received a clock tick event!
Received a clock tick event!
Press any key to continue

Each message is printed with a delay of one second and five messages are printed in total.

> **Multicast events**

Since events are implemented as multicast delegates in C#, we can subscribe multiple event handlers to a single event. For example, consider this revised Test class:

```
class Test
{
    static void Main()
    {
        ClockTimer clockTimer = new ClockTimer();
        clockTimer.Timer += new TimerEvent(OnClockTick);
        clockTimer.Timer += new TimerEvent(OnClockTick2);
        clockTimer.Start();
    }
    public static void OnClockTick(object sender, EventArgs e)
    {
        Console.WriteLine("Received a clock tick event!");
    }
    public static void OnClockTick2(object sender, EventArgs e)
    {
        Console.WriteLine("Received a clock tick event in OnClockTick2!");
    }
}
```

}

Here we have introduced another event handler, 'OnClockTick2', and have subscribed it also to the Timer event in the Main() method using the '+=' operator. The output of this program is:

Received a clock tick event!
Received a clock tick event in OnClockTick2!
Received a clock tick event!
Received a clock tick event in OnClockTick2!
Received a clock tick event!
Received a clock tick event in OnClockTick2!
Received a clock tick event!
Received a clock tick event in OnClockTick2!
Received a clock tick event!
Received a clock tick event in OnClockTick2!
Press any key to continue

As can be seen in the output above, now both the OnClockTick() and OnClockTick2() are invoked each time the event is raised.

> **Passing some data with the Event: Sub-classing System.EventArgs**

Finally, we can pass some additional information while raising an event. For this, we need to perform the following three steps: 1. Define a class that inherits from System.EventArgs 2. Encapsulate the data to be passed with the event within this class (preferably using properties) 3. Create an instance of this class in the event generator class and pass it with the event

Let's now change our previous Clock Timer example so that the event raised also contains the sequence number of the clock ticks. First we need to define a new class 'ClockTimerArgs', which inherits from the System.EventArgs class.

```
public class ClockTimerArgs : EventArgs
{
    private int tickCount;
    public ClockTimerArgs(int tickCount)
    {
        this.tickCount = tickCount;
    }
    public int TickCount
    {
        get { return tickCount; }
    }
}
```

The ClockTimerArgs class contains a private variable named 'tickCount' to hold the current tick number. This value is passed to the object through a public constructor and is accessible to the event handler through the public property. Next we need to change the delegate definition for the event to:

public delegate void TimerEvent(object sender, ClockTimerArgs e);

The argument type in the delegate is changed from EventArgs to ClockTimerArgs so that the publisher (event generator) can pass this particular type of arguments to the subscriber (event handler). The event generator class is defined as:

```
class ClockTimer
{
    public event TimerEvent Timer;
    public void Start()
    {
        for(int i=0; i<5; i++)
        {
            Timer(this, new ClockTimerArgs(i+1));
            Thread.Sleep(1000);
        }
    }
}
```

The only change in this class is that instead of passing null as the second argument, we are passing a new object of the ClockTimerArgs type with the sequence number of the current clock tick.

Finally, the event handler is written:

```
public static void OnClockTick(object sender, ClockTimerArgs e)
{
    Console.WriteLine("Received a clock tick event. This is clock tick
    number {0}", e.TickCount);
}
```

Here we have simply printed the clock tick number using the ClockTimerArgs' TickCount Property. The complete source code is shown below.

```
using System;
using System.Threading;
namespace CSharpSchool
{
    class Test
    {
        static void Main()
        {
            ClockTimer clockTimer = new ClockTimer();
            clockTimer.Timer += new TimerEvent(OnClockTick);
            clockTimer.Start();
        }
        public static void OnClockTick(object sender, ClockTimerArgs e)
        {
            Console.WriteLine("Received a clock tick event. This
            is clock tick number {0}", e.TickCount);
        }
    }
    public class ClockTimerArgs : EventArgs
    {
        private int tickCount;
        public ClockTimerArgs(int tickCount)
        {
            this.tickCount = tickCount;
        }
        public int TickCount
        {
            get { return tickCount; }
        }
    }
```

```
}
public delegate void TimerEvent(object sender, ClockTimerArgs e);

class ClockTimer
{
    public event TimerEvent Timer;
    public void Start()
    {
        for(int i=0; i<5; i++)
        {
            Timer(this, new ClockTimerArgs(i+1));
            Thread.Sleep(1000);
        }
    }
}
}
```

When the above program is compiled and executed, we will see the following output:

Received a clock tick event. This is clock tick number 1
Received a clock tick event. This is clock tick number 2
Received a clock tick event. This is clock tick number 3
Received a clock tick event. This is clock tick number 4
Received a clock tick event. This is clock tick number 5
Press any key to continue

As the output of the program illustrates, now we are also receiving the clock tick number along with each event.

Chapter 5: Multithreading in C#

❖ **Thread**

A thread is an independent stream of instructions in a program. All your C# programs up to this point have one entry point — the Main() method. Execution starts with the first statement in the Main() method and continues until that method returns.

➤ **What is Multithreading**

Multithreading is a feature provided by the operating system that enables your application to have more than one execution path at the same time. We are all used to Windows' multitasking abilities, which allow us to execute more than one application at the same time. Suppose you are writing the any document in Microsoft Word, listening to your favorite songs in Winamp and downloading a new song using Internet Download Manager. In a similar manner, you may use multithreading to run different methods of our program at the same time. Multithreading is such a common element of today's programming that it is difficult to find windows applications that don't use it. For example, Microsoft Word takes user input and displays it on the screen in one thread while it continues to check spelling and grammatical mistakes in the second thread, and at the same time the third thread saves the document automatically at regular intervals. In a similar manner, WinAmp plays music in one thread, displays visualizations in the second and takes user input in the third. This is quite different from multitasking as here a single application is doing multiple tasks at the same time, while in multitasking different applications execute at the same time.

Note :

When we say two or more applications or threads are running at the same time, we mean that they appear to execute at the same time, e.g. without one waiting for the termination of the other before starting. Technically, no two instructions can execute together at the same time on a single processor system (which most of us use). What the operating system does is divides the processor's execution time amongst the different applications (multitasking) and within an application amongst the different threads (multithreading).

Just consider the following small program:

```
namespace CSharpSchool
{
        class Test
        {
                static void Main()
                {
                        Fun1();
                        Fun2();
                        Console.WriteLine("End of Main()");
                }
                public static void Fun1()
                {
                        for(int i=1; i<=5; i++)
                        {
                                Console.WriteLine("Fun1() writes: {0}", i);
                        }
                }
                public static void Fun2()
```

```
{
        for(int i=10; i>=6; i--)
        {
                Console.WriteLine("Fun2() writes: {0}", i);
        }
    }
}
}
```

The output of the program is:

```
Fun1() writes: 1
Fun1() writes: 2
Fun1() writes: 3
Fun1() writes: 4
Fun1() writes: 5
Fun2() writes: 10
Fun2() writes: 9
Fun2() writes: 8
Fun2() writes: 7
Fun2() writes: 6
End of Main()
```

As we can see, the method Fun2() only started its execution when Fun1() had completed its execution. This is because when a method gets called, the execution control transfers to that method, and when the method returns the execution starts from the very next line of the code that called the method, i.e., the program implicitly has only one execution path. Using multithreading, we can define multiple concurrent execution paths within our program called threads. For example, we can use threads so that the two methods Fun1() and Fun2() may execute without waiting for each other to terminate.

➢ **MultiThreading in C#**

The .Net Framework, and thus C#, provides full support for multiple execution threads in a program. You can add threading functionality to your application by using the System.Threading namespace. A thread in .Net is represented by the System.Threading.Thread class. We can create multiple threads in our program by creating multiple instances (objects) of this class. A thread starts its execution by calling the specified method and terminates when the execution of that method gets completed. We can specify the method name that the thread will call when it starts by passing a delegate of the ThreadStart type in the Thread class constructor. The delegate System.Threading.ThreadStart may reference any method with has the void return type and which takes no arguments.

public delegate void ThreadStart();

For example, we can change our previous application to run the two methods in two different threads like this:

Thread firstThread = new Thread(new ThreadStart(Fun1));
Thread secondThread = new Thread(new ThreadStart(Fun2));

Here we have created two instances of the Thread class and passed a ThreadStart type delegate in the constructor which references a method in our program. It is important that the method referenced in the Thread class constructor, through the ThreadStart delegate, is parameterless and has void return type. A thread does not start its execution when its object is created.

Rather, we have to start the execution of a thread by calling the Start() method of the Thread class.

firstThread.Start();
secondThread.Start();

Here we have called the Start() method of firstThread, which in turn will call the Fun1() method in a new thread. However this time the execution will not halt until the completion of the Fun1() method, but will immediately continue with the next statement which also starts the execution of Fun2() method in a new thread. Again, the main thread of our application will not wait for the completion of the Fun2() method and will continue with the following statement. The complete source code for the application is:

```
using System;
using System.Threading;
namespace CSharpSchool
{
        class Test
        {
                static void Main()
                {
                        Thread firstThread = new Thread(new ThreadStart(Fun1));
                        Thread secondThread = new Thread(new ThreadStart(Fun2));
                        firstThread.Start();
                        secondThread.Start();
                        Console.WriteLine("End of Main()");
                }
                public static void Fun1()
                {
                        for(int i=1; i<=5; i++)
                        {
                                Console.WriteLine("Fun1() writes: {0}", i);
                        }
                }
                public static void Fun2()
                {
                        for(int i=10; i>=6; i--)
                        {
                                Console.WriteLine("Fun2() writes: {0}", i);
                        }
                }
        }
}
```

One possible output of the program is:

```
End of Main()
Fun1() writes: 1
Fun1() writes: 2
Fun1() writes: 3
Fun1() writes: 4
Fun1() writes: 5
Fun2() writes: 10
Fun2() writes: 9
Fun2() writes: 8
Fun2() writes: 7
Fun2() writes: 6
```

C# Programming Made Easy

Why did we say 'one possible output'? The reason is that we can't be sure about the execution sequence of the threads. Thread switching is completely Operating System dependent and may change each time you execute the program. Here what we notice is that the Main() thread ended before the start of any of the other two threads, but after that the two functions seem to be calling in a sequence. What we might have expected was loop iterations of the two methods coming in a mixed way. So why didn't we get that output? In fact, the methods Fun1() and Fun2() have such short execution times that they get finished even before the switching of the two threads for a single time. If we increase the loop counters of these methods, we may notice the threads in execution.

> **Instance members of the System.Threaing.Thread class**

The most commonly used instance members of the thread class are:

Member	Description
Name	A property of string type used to get/set the friendly name of the thread instance.
Priority	A property of type System.Threading.ThreadPriority. This property is use to get/set the value indicating the scheduling priority of the thread. The priority can be any instance of the ThreadPriority enumeration which includes AboveNormal, BelowNormal, Normal, Highest and Lowest.
IsAlive	A Boolean property indicating whether the thread is alive or has been terminated.
ThreadState	A property of type System.Threading.ThreadState. This property is used to get the value containing the state of the thread. The value returned by this property is an instance of the ThreadState enumeration which includes Aborted, AbortRequested, Suspended, Stopped, Unstarted, Running, WaitSleepJoin, etc
Start()	Starts the execution of the thread
Abort()	Allows the current thread to stop the execution of a thread permanently. The method throws the ThreadAbortException in the executing thread.
Suspend()	Pauses the execution of a thread temporarily
Resume()	Resumes the execution of a suspended thread
Join()	Makes the current thread wait for another thread to finish

> **Thread Demonstration Example - Basic Operations**

Now we will start to understand the implementation of threads in C#. Consider the following C# Console program:

```
using System;
using System.Threading;
namespace CSharpSchool
{
  class Test
  {
    static Thread mainThread;
    static Thread firstThread;
    static Thread secondThread;
    static void Main()
    {
      mainThread = Thread.CurrentThread;
      firstThread = new Thread(new ThreadStart(Fun1));
      secondThread = new Thread(new ThreadStart(Fun2));
      mainThread.Name = "Main Thread";
```

```
    firstThread.Name = "First Thread";
    secondThread.Name = "Second Thread";
    ThreadsInfo("Main() before starting the threads");
    firstThread.Start();
    secondThread.Start();
    ThreadsInfo("Main() just before exiting the Main()");
}
public static void ThreadsInfo(string location)
{
    Console.WriteLine("\r\n\n {0}", location);
    Console.WriteLine("Thread Name: {0}, ThreadState: {1}",
    mainThread.Name, mainThread.ThreadState);
    Console.WriteLine("Thread Name: {0}, ThreadState: {1}",
    firstThread.Name, firstThread.ThreadState);
    Console.WriteLine("Thread Name: {0}, ThreadState: {1}\r\n",
    secondThread.Name, secondThread.ThreadState);
}
public static void Fun1()
{
    for(int i=1; i<=5; i++)
    {
        Console.WriteLine("Fun1() writes: {0}", i);
        Thread.Sleep(100);
    }
    ThreadsInfo("Fun1()");
}
public static void Fun2()
{
    for(int i=10; i>=6; i--)
    {
        Console.WriteLine("Fun2() writes: {0}", i);
        Thread.Sleep(125);
    }
    ThreadsInfo("Fun2()");
  }
 }
}
```

First of all we have defined three static references of type System.Threading.Thread to reference the three threads (main, first and second thread) later in the Main() method:

static Thread mainThread;
static Thread firstThread;
static Thread secondThread;

We have defined a static method called ThreadsInfo() to display the information (name and state) of the three threads. The two methods Fun1() and Fun2() are similar to the previous program and just print 5 numbers. In the loop of these methods we have called the Sleep() method which will make the thread executing the method suspend for the specified amount of time. We have set slightly different times in each the threads' Sleep() methods. After the loop, we have printed the information about all the threads again.

```
    public static void Fun2()
    {
        for(int i=10; i>=6; i--)
        {
            Console.WriteLine("Fun2() writes: {0}", i);
```

```
            Thread.Sleep(125);
        }
        ThreadsInfo("Fun2()");
    }
```

Inside the Main() method we first instantiated the two thread instances (firstThread and secondThread) by passing to the constructors the references of the Fun1() and Fun2() methods respectively using the ThreadStart delegate. We also made the reference mainThread point to the thread executing the Main() method by using the Thread.CurrentThread property in the Main() method.

```
static void Main()
{
    mainThread = Thread.CurrentThread;
    firstThread = new Thread(new ThreadStart(Fun1));
    secondThread = new Thread(new ThreadStart(Fun2));
```

We then set the Name property of these threads to the threads corresponding names.

```
    mainThread.Name = "Main Thread";
    firstThread.Name = "First Thread";
    secondThread.Name = "Second Thread";
```

After setting the names, we printed the current state of the three threads by calling the static ThreadsInfo() method, started the two threads and finally called the ThreadsInfo() method just before the end of the Main() method.

```
    ThreadsInfo("Main() before starting the threads");
    firstThread.Start();
    secondThread.Start();
    ThreadsInfo("Main() just before exiting the Main()");
```

One possible output of the program is:

In Main() before starting the threads
Thread Name: Main Thread, ThreadState: Running
Thread Name: First Thread, ThreadState: Unstarted
Thread Name: Second Thread, ThreadState: Unstarted

In Main() just before exiting the Main()
Thread Name: Main Thread, ThreadState: Running
Thread Name: First Thread, ThreadState: Unstarted
Thread Name: Second Thread, ThreadState: Unstarted

Fun1() writes: 1
Fun2() writes: 10
Fun1() writes: 2
Fun2() writes: 9
Fun1() writes: 3
Fun2() writes: 8
Fun1() writes: 4
Fun2() writes: 7

Fun1() writes: 5

In Fun1()
Thread Name: Main Thread, ThreadState: Background, Stopped, WaitSleepJoin
Thread Name: First Thread, ThreadState: Running
Thread Name: Second Thread, ThreadState: WaitSleepJoin

Fun2() writes: 6

In Fun2()
Thread Name: Main Thread, ThreadState: Background, Stopped, WaitSleepJoin
Thread Name: First Thread, ThreadState: Stopped
Thread Name: Second Thread, ThreadState: Running

The important thing to note here is the sequence of execution and the thread states at different points during the execution of the program. The two threads (firstThread and secondThread) didn't get started even when the Main() method was exiting. At the end of firstThread, the Main() thread has stopped while the secondThread is in the Sleep state.

➢ Passing Data to Threads

There are two ways to pass some data to a thread. You can either use the Thread constructor with the ParameterizedThreadStart delegate, or you can create a custom class and define the method of the thread as an instance method so that you can initialize data of the instance before starting the thread. For passing data to a thread, any class or struct that holds the data is needed. Here, the struct Data containing a string is defined, but you can pass any object you want:

```
public struct Data
{
        public string Message;
}
```

If the ParameterizedThreadStart delegate is used, the entry point of the thread must have a parameter of type object and a void return type. The object can be cast to what it is, and here the message is written to the console:

```
static void ThreadMainWithParameters(object o)
{
        Data d = (Data)o;
        Console.WriteLine("Running in a thread, received {0}", d.Message);
}
```

With the constructor of the Thread class, you can assign the new entry point ThreadMainWithParameters and invoke the Start() method passing the variable d :

```
static void Main()
{
        Data d = new Data();
        d.Message = "Info";
        Thread t2 = new Thread(ThreadMainWithParameters);
        t2.Start(d);
}
```

Another way to pass data to the new thread is to define a class (see the class MyThread), where you define the fields that are needed as well as the main method of the thread as an instance method of the class:

```csharp
public class MyThread
{
    private string data;
    public MyThread(string data)
    {
        this.data = data;
    }
    public void ThreadMain()
    {
        Console.WriteLine("Running in a thread, data: {0}", data);
    }
}
```

This way, you can create an object of MyThread , and pass the object and the method ThreadMain() to the constructor of the Thread class. The thread can access the data.

```csharp
MyThread obj = new MyThread("info");
Thread t3 = new Thread(obj.ThreadMain);
t3.Start();
```

➢ **Background Threads**

The process of the application keeps running as long as at least one foreground thread is running. If more than one foreground thread is running and the Main() method ends, the process of the application keeps active until all foreground threads finish their work.

A thread you create with the Thread class, by default, is a foreground thread. Thread pool threads are always background threads. When you create a thread with the Thread class, you can define whether it should be a foreground or background thread by setting the property IsBackground . The Main() method sets the IsBackground property of the thread t1 to false (which is the default). After starting the new thread, the main thread just writes to the console an end message. The new thread writes a start and an end message, and in between it sleeps for 3 seconds. The 3 seconds provide a good chance for the main thread to finish before the new thread completes its work.

```csharp
class Program
{
    static void Main()
    {
        Thread t1 = new Thread(ThreadMain);
        t1.Name = "MyNewThread1";
        t1.IsBackground = false;
        t1.Start();
        Console.WriteLine("Main thread ending now...");
    }
    static void ThreadMain()
    {
        Console.WriteLine("Thread {0} started", Thread.CurrentThread.Name);
        Thread.Sleep(3000);
        Console.WriteLine("Thread                {0}                completed", Thread.CurrentThread.Name);
    }
```

}

When you start the application, you will still see the completion message written to the console, although the main thread completed its work earlier. The reason is that the new thread is a foreground thread as well.

Main thread ending now...
Thread MyNewThread1 started
Thread MyNewThread1 completed

If you change the IsBackground property to start the new thread to true , the result shown at the console is different. You can have the same result as shown here — the start message of the new thread is shown but never the end message. You might not see the start message either, if the thread was prematurely ended before it had a chance to kick off.

Main thread ending now...
Thread MyNewThread1 started

Background threads are very useful for background tasks. For example, when you close the Word application, it doesn ' t make sense for the spell checker to keep its process running. The spell checker thread can be killed when the application is closed. However, the thread organizing the Outlook message store should remain active until it is finished even if Outlook is closed.

➤ **Thread Priority**

When two or more threads are executing simultaneously they share the processor time. In normal conditions, the operating system tries to distribute the processor time equally amongst the threads of a process. However, if we wish to influence how processor time is distributed, we can also specify the priority level for our threads. In .Net we do this using the System.Threading.ThreadPriority enumeration, which contains Normal, AboveNormal, BelowNormal, Highest and Lowest. The default priority level of a thread is, to no one's surprise, Normal. A thread with a higher priority is given more time by Operating System than a thread with a lower priority. Consider the program below with no priority setting:

```
class Test
{
        static void Main()
        {
                Thread firstThread = new Thread(new ThreadStart(Fun1));
                Thread secondThread = new Thread(new ThreadStart(Fun2));
                firstThread.Name = "First Thread";
                secondThread.Name = "Second Thread";

                firstThread.Start();
                secondThread.Start();
        }
        public static void Fun1()
        {
                for(int i=1; i<=10; i++)
                {
                        int t = new Random().Next(20);
                        for(int j=0; j<t; j++)
                        {
                                new String(new char[] {});
                        }
                }
```

```
            Console.WriteLine(Thread.CurrentThread.Name +
        ": created: " + t.ToString() + " empty strings");
        }
    }
    public static void Fun2()
    {
        for(int i=20; i>=11; i--)
        {
            int t = new Random().Next(20);
            for(int j=0; j<t; j++)
            {
                new String(new char[] {});
            }
            Console.WriteLine(Thread.CurrentThread.Name +
        ": created: " + t.ToString()
        + "empty strings");
        }
    }
}
```

Here we have asked the runtime to create an almost similar number of objects in the two thread methods (Fun1() and Fun2()). One possible output of the program is:

First Thread: created: 18 empty strings
First Thread: created: 5 empty strings
First Thread: created: 5 empty strings
First Thread: created: 5 empty strings
First Thread: created: 5 empty strings
First Thread: created: 5 empty strings
First Thread: created: 5 empty strings
First Thread: created: 5 empty strings
First Thread: created: 5 empty strings
First Thread: created: 5 empty strings
Second Thread: created: 16 empty strings
Second Thread: created: 5 empty strings
Second Thread: created: 5 empty strings
Second Thread: created: 5 empty strings
Second Thread: created: 5 empty strings
Second Thread: created: 5 empty strings
Second Thread: created: 5 empty strings
Second Thread: created: 5 empty strings
Second Thread: created: 5 empty strings
Second Thread: created: 5 empty strings

Now we will change the priority of secondThread to AboveNormal:

```
class Test
{
    static void Main()
    {
        Thread firstThread = new Thread(new ThreadStart(Fun1));
        Thread secondThread = new Thread(new ThreadStart(Fun2));
        firstThread.Name = "First Thread";
        secondThread.Name = "Second Thread";
        secondThread.Priority = ThreadPriority.AboveNormal;

        firstThread.Start();
```

```
            secondThread.Start();
    }
    public static void Fun1()
    {
            for(int i=1; i<=10; i++)
            {
                    int t = new Random().Next(20);
                    for(int j=0; j<t; j++)
                    {
                            new String(new char[] {});
                    }
                    Console.WriteLine(Thread.CurrentThread.Name +
            ": created: " + t.ToString() + " empty strings");
            }
    }
    public static void Fun2()
    {
            for(int i=20; i>=11; i--)
            {
                    int t = new Random().Next(40);
                    for(int j=0; j<t; j++)
                    {
                            new String(new char[] {});
                    }
                    Console.WriteLine(Thread.CurrentThread.Name +
            ": created: " + t.ToString() + " empty strings");
            }
    }
}
```

Here we have made two changes. We have increased the priority of the secondThread to AboveNormal. We have also increased the range for random numbers so that the second thread would be required to create a greater number of objects. On compiling and executing the program, we get output like:

```
Second Thread: created: 14 empty strings
Second Thread: created: 18 empty strings
Second Thread: created: 18 empty strings
Second Thread: created: 18 empty strings
Second Thread: created: 27 empty strings
Second Thread: created: 27 empty strings
Second Thread: created: 27 empty strings
Second Thread: created: 27 empty strings
Second Thread: created: 27 empty strings
Second Thread: created: 27 empty strings
First Thread: created: 13 empty strings
First Thread: created: 13 empty strings
First Thread: created: 13 empty strings
First Thread: created: 13 empty strings
First Thread: created: 13 empty strings
First Thread: created: 13 empty strings
First Thread: created: 13 empty strings
First Thread: created: 13 empty strings
First Thread: created: 13 empty strings
First Thread: created: 13 empty strings
Press any key to continue
```

Consider the above output. Although the second thread is creating more objects, it still finishes before the first thread. The reason simply is that now the priority level of second thread is higher than that of the first thread.

> **Thread Execution Control**

The Thread class also provides methods for controlling the execution of different threads. You can start, stop (called abort), suspend and resume suspended threads just by calling a single method on the Thread object. Consider the following demonstration application:

```
static void Main()
{
        Thread firstThread = new Thread(new ThreadStart(Fun1));
        firstThread.Start();
        Console.WriteLine("Thread started");
        Thread.Sleep(150);
        firstThread.Suspend();
        Console.WriteLine("Thread suspended");
        Thread.Sleep(150);
        firstThread.Resume();
        Console.WriteLine("Thread resumed");
        Thread.Sleep(150);
        firstThread.Abort();
        Console.WriteLine("Thread aborted");
}
public static void Fun1()
{
        int i=1;
        try
        {
                for(; i<=20; i++)
                {
                        int t = new Random().Next(20, 50);
                        Console.WriteLine("Thread 1: slept for: " +
                t.ToString() + " milliseconds");
                        Thread.Sleep(t);
                }
        }
        catch(ThreadAbortException ex)
        {
                Console.WriteLine("Thread 1 aborted in iteration number: {0}", i);
        }
}
```

Here we have started, suspended, resumed and aborted the thread (firstThread) with a constant difference of 150 milliseconds. Remember that when a thread is aborted the runtime throws the ThreadAbortException in the thread method. This exception allows our thread to perform some cleanup work before it's termination, e.g. closing the opened database, network or file connections. When we execute the above program, we see the following output:

Thread started
Thread 1: slept for: 35 milliseconds
Thread 1: slept for: 29 milliseconds
Thread 1: slept for: 49 milliseconds
Thread 1: slept for: 36 milliseconds

Thread 1: slept for: 33 milliseconds
Thread 1: slept for: 30 milliseconds
Thread suspended
Thread resumed
Thread 1: slept for: 44 milliseconds
Thread 1: slept for: 48 milliseconds
Thread aborted
Press any key to continue

Note that there is no thread activity between thread suspend and resume.

A word of caution: If you try to call the Suspend(), Resume() or Abort() methods on a non-running thread (aborted or un-started), you will get the ThreadStateException.

> **Using Join() to wait for running threads**

Finally, you can make a thread wait for other running threads to complete by calling the Join() method. Consider this simple code:

```
static void Main()
{
        Thread firstThread = new Thread(new ThreadStart(Fun1));
        Thread secondThread = new Thread(new ThreadStart(Fun2));
        firstThread.Start();
        secondThread.Start();
        Console.WriteLine("Ending Main()");
}
public static void Fun1()
{
        for(int i=1; i<=5; i++)
        {
                Console.WriteLine("Thread 1 writes: {0}", i);
        }
}
public static void Fun2()
{
        for(int i=10; i>=5; i--)
        {
                Console.WriteLine("Thread 2 writes: {0}", i);
        }
}
```

In the above code, the thread of the Main() method will terminate quickly after starting the two threads. The output of the program will look like this:

Thread 1 writes: 1
Thread 2 writes: 10
Ending Main()
Thread 1 writes: 2
Thread 1 writes: 3
Thread 1 writes: 4
Thread 1 writes: 5
Thread 2 writes: 9

Thread 2 writes: 8
Thread 2 writes: 7
Thread 2 writes: 6
Thread 2 writes: 5
Press any key to continue

But if we like to keep our Main() thread alive until the first thread is alive, we can apply Join() method to it.

```
static void Main()
{
        Thread firstThread = new Thread(new ThreadStart(Fun1));
        Thread secondThread = new Thread(new ThreadStart(Fun2));
        firstThread.Start();
        secondThread.Start();
        firstThread.Join();
        Console.WriteLine("Ending Main()");
}
public static void Fun1()
{
        for(int i=1; i<=5; i++)
        {
                Console.WriteLine("Thread 1 writes: {0}", i);
        }
}
public static void Fun2()
{
        for(int i=15; i>=6; i--)
        {
                Console.WriteLine("Thread 2 writes: {0}", i);
        }
}
```

Here we have inserted the call to the Join() method of firstThread and increased the loop counter for secondThread. Now the Main() method thread will not terminate until the first thread is alive. One possible output of the program is:

Thread 1 writes: 1
Thread 1 writes: 2
Thread 1 writes: 3
Thread 1 writes: 4
Thread 1 writes: 5
Ending Main()
Thread 2 writes: 15
Thread 2 writes: 14
Thread 2 writes: 13
Thread 2 writes: 12
Thread 2 writes: 11
Thread 2 writes: 10
Thread 2 writes: 9
Thread 2 writes: 8
Thread 2 writes: 7
Thread 2 writes: 6

Note: Since our threads are doing such little work, you might not get the exact output. You may get the Main() thread exiting at the end of both the threads. To see the real effect of threads competition, increase the loop counters to hundreds in the examples of this lesson.

C# Programming Made Easy

> **Synchronization**

So far we have seen the positive aspects of using multiple threads. In all of the programs presented so far, the threads of a program were not sharing any common resources (objects). The threads were using only the local variables of their corresponding methods. But what happens when multiple threads try to access the same shared resource? suppose thread 1 gets a DataRow from a DataTable and starts updating its column values. At the same time, thread 2 starts and also accesses the same DataRow object to update its column values. Both the threads save the data row back to the table and physical database. But which data row version has been saved to the database? The one updated by thread 1 or the one updated by thread 2? We can't predict the actual result with any certainty. It can be the one update by thread 1 or the one update by thread 2 or it may be the mixture of both of these updates... Who will like to have such a situation?

So what is the solution? Well the simplest solution is not to use shared objects with multiple threads. This might sound funny, but this is what most the programmers practice. They avoid using shared objects with multiple threads executing simultaneously. But in some cases, it is desirable to use shared objects with multiple threads. .Net provides a locking mechanism to avoid accidental simultaneous access by multiple threads to the same shared object.

> **The C# Locking Mechanism**

```
class Test
{
        static StringBuilder text = new StringBuilder();
        static void Main()
        {
                Thread firstThread = new Thread(new ThreadStart(Fun1));
                Thread secondThread = new Thread(new ThreadStart(Fun2));
                firstThread.Start();
                secondThread.Start();
                firstThread.Join();
                secondThread.Join();
                Console.WriteLine("Text is:\r\n{0}", text.ToString());
        }
        public static void Fun1()
        {
                for(int i=1; i<=20; i++)
                {
                        Thread.Sleep(10);
                        text.Append(i.ToString() + " ");
                }
        }
        public static void Fun2()
        {
                for(int i=21; i<=40; i++)
                {
                        Thread.Sleep(2);
                        text.Append(i.ToString() + " ");
                }
        }
}
```

Both the threads are appending numbers to the shared string builder (System.Text.StringBuilder) object. As a result in the output, the final string would be something like:

Text is:
21 1 22 2 23 3 24 4 25 5 26 6 27 7 28 8 29 9 10 30 31 11
32 12 33 13 34 14 35 15 36 16 37 17 38 18 39 19 40 20
Press any key to continue

The final text is an unordered sequence of numbers. To avoid threads interfering with each others results, each thread should lock the shared object before it starts appending the numbers and release the lock when it is done. While the object is locked, no other thread should be allowed to change the state of the object. This is exactly what the C# lock keyword does. We can change the above program to provide the locking functionality:

```
class Test
{
        static StringBuilder text = new StringBuilder();
        static void Main()
        {
                Thread firstThread = new Thread(new ThreadStart(Fun1));
                Thread secondThread = new Thread(new ThreadStart(Fun2));
                firstThread.Start();
                secondThread.Start();
                firstThread.Join();
                secondThread.Join();
                Console.WriteLine("Text is:\r\n{0}", text.ToString());
        }
        public static void Fun1()
        {
                lock(text)
                {
                        for(int i=1; i<=20; i++)
                        {
                                Thread.Sleep(10);
                                text.Append(i.ToString() + " ");
                        }
                }
        }
        public static void Fun2()
        {
                lock(text)
                {
                        for(int i=21; i<=40; i++)
                        {
                                Thread.Sleep(2);
                                text.Append(i.ToString() + " ");
                        }
                }
        }
}
```

Note that now each thread is locking the shared object 'text' before working on it. Hence, the output of the program will be:

Text is:
1 2 3 4 5 6 7 8 9 10 11 12 13 14 15 16 17 18 19 20 21 22
23 24 25 26 27 28 29 30 31 32 33 34 35 36 37 38 39 40

Press any key to continue

Or,

Text is:
21 22 23 24 25 26 27 28 29 30 31 32 33 34 35 36 37 38
39 40 1 2 3 4 5 6 7 8 9 10 11 12 13 14 15 16 17 18 19 20
Press any key to continue

You will see the first output when the firstThread will succeed to lock the 'text' object first while the second output shows that the secondThread has succeeded in locking the 'text' object first.

> **Deadlock**

Another issue regarding thread synchronization is deadlock. Consider there are two shared objects A and B. Thread 1 first locks A and then B

```
// code for Thread 1
lock(A)
{
        lock(B)
        {
                // do some work
        }
}
```

While the second thread locks B and then A

```
// code for Thread 2
lock(B)
{
        lock(A)
        {
                // do some work
        }
}
```

Suppose the two threads start at the same time and following execution sequence is generated by the Operating System

    * Thread 1 takes lock on A
    * Thread 2 takes lock on B
    * Thread 1 waits for the lock on B held by Thread 2...
    * Thread 2 waits for the lock on A held by Thread 1...

Thread 1 will not leave the lock on A until it has got the lock on B and has finished its work. On the other hand, Thread 2 will not leave the lock on B until it has got the lock on A and has finished its work, which will never happen! Hence the program will be deadlocked at this stage. How to avoid deadlock is a matter of extensive research. These kinds of deadlocks also occur in database servers and operating systems. Hence, one must be very careful when using multiple locks. This kind of bugs are really very hard to detect and correct as there is no exception thrown and no error is reported at runtime; the program just stops responding, leaving you in an abysmal situation. To experience a deadlock yourself, compile and execute the following program.

```csharp
using System;
using System.Threading;
using System.Text;
namespace CSharpSchool
{
    class Test
    {
        static StringBuilder text = new StringBuilder();
        static StringBuilder doc = new StringBuilder();
        static void Main()
        {
            Thread firstThread = new Thread(new ThreadStart(Fun1));
            Thread secondThread = new Thread(new ThreadStart(Fun2));
            firstThread.Start();
            secondThread.Start();
        }
        public static void Fun1()
        {
            lock(text)
            {
                Thread.Sleep(10);
                for(int i=1; i<=20; i++)
                {
                    text.Append(i.ToString() + " ");
                }
                lock(doc)
                {
                    doc.Append(text.ToString());
                    for(int i=1; i<=20; i++)
                    {
                        doc.Append(i.ToString() + " ");
                    }
                }
            }
        }
        public static void Fun2()
        {
            lock(doc)
            {
                Thread.Sleep(10);
                for(int i=21; i<=40; i++)
                {
                    doc.Append(i.ToString() + " ");
                }
                lock(text)
                {
                    text.Append(doc.ToString());
                    for(int i=21; i<=40; i++)
                    {
                        text.Append(i.ToString() + " ");
                    }
                }
            }
        }
    }
}
```

C# Programming Made Easy

Here we have used two shared objects (text and doc). Both the threads are attempting to lock the two objects in the opposite order. If in a particular run, both the threads lock their first object at the same time, a deadlock is bound to occur. You might not find any deadlock in the first run. But on executing the program again and again, you will surely come up against a deadlocked situation. In this case, the program will hang and stop responding.

Chapter 6: Collection & Generics

❖ Collections

Although we can make collections of related objects using arrays, there are some limitations when using arrays for collections. The size of an array is always fixed and must be defined at the time of instantiation of an array. Secondly, an array can only contain objects of the same data type, which we need to define at the time of its instantiation. Also, an array does not impose any particular mechanism for inserting and retrieving the elements of a collection. For this purpose, the creators of C# and the .Net Framework Class Library (FCL) have provided a number of classes to serve as a collection of different types. These classes are present in the System.Collections namespace.

At the beginning we will see the foundation on which each collection class lies. It's really important to understand the interface on which they are based: IEnumerable and its ICollections extension. From the latter there are two other interfaces derived: IList and IDictionary. The collections classes which are built into the System.Collections namespaces are always implementing each of the aforementioned interfaces. However, keep in mind that there are other interfaces too (e.g.; IEnumerator, IComparer, etc.).

Some of the most common classes from this namespace are:

Class	Description
ArrayList	Provides a collection similar to an array, but that grows dynamically as the number of elements change.
Stack	A collection that works on the Last In First Out (LIFO) principle, i.e., the last item inserted is the first item removed from the collection.
Queue	A collection that works on the First In First Out (FIFO) principle, i.e., the first item inserted is the first item removed from the collection.
Hashtable	Provides a collection of key-value pairs that are organized based on the hash code of the key.
SortedList	Provides a collection of key-value pairs where the items are sorted according to the key. The items are accessible by both the keys and the index.
BitArray	The BitArray class manages a compact array of bit values. These bit values are boolean in nature, having the value true (1) or false (0).

➢ ArrayList

The System.Collections.ArrayList class is similar to arrays, but can store elements of any data type. We don't need to specify the size of the collection when using an ArrayList (as we used to do in the case of simple arrays). The size of the ArrayList grows dynamically as the number of elements it contains changes. An ArrayList uses an array internally and initializes its size with a default value called Capacity. As the number of elements increase or decrease, ArrayList adjusts the capacity of the array accordingly by making a new array and copying the old values into it. The Size of the ArrayList is the total number of elements that are actually present in it while the

Capacity is the number of elements the ArrayList can hold without instantiating a new array. An ArrayList can be constructed like this:

```
ArrayList list = new ArrayList();
```

We can also specify the initial Capacity of the ArrayList by passing an integer value to the constructor:

```
ArrayList list = new ArrayList(20);
```

We can also create an ArrayList with some other collection by passing the collection in the constructor:

```
ArrayList list = new ArrayList(someCollection);
```

We add elements to the ArrayList by using its Add() method. The Add() method takes an object of type object as its parameter.

```
list.Add(45);
list.Add(87);
list.Add(12);
```

This will add the three numbers to the ArrayList. Now, we can iterate through the items in the ArrayList (list) using a foreach loop:

```
static void Main()
{
        ArrayList list = new ArrayList();
        list.Add(45);
        list.Add(87);
        list.Add(12);
        foreach(int num in list)
        {
                Console.WriteLine(num);
        }
}
```

which will print out the elements in the ArrayList as

```
45
87
12
```

The ArrayList class has also implemented the indexer property (or index operator) which allow its elements to be accessed using the [] operators, just as you do with a simple array (we will see how to implement indexers in the next lesson). The following code is similar to the above code but uses the indexers to access the elements of the ArrayList.

```
static void Main()
{
        ArrayList list = new ArrayList();
        list.Add(45);
        list.Add(87);
        list.Add(12);
        for(int i=0; i<list.Count; i++)
        {
```

```
        Console.WriteLine(list[i]);
    }
}
```

The output of the code will be similar to the one presented previously. The above code uses the property Count to find the current number of elements in the ArrayList. Recall that ArrayList inherits this property (Count) from its parent interface ICollection.

A list of some other important properties and methods of the ArrayList class is presented in the following table:

Methods

Name	Description
Add	Adds an object to the end of the ArrayList.
AddRange	Adds the elements of an ICollection to the end of the ArrayList.
BinarySearch(Object)	Searches the entire sorted ArrayList for an element using the default comparer and returns the zero-based index of the element.
Clear	Removes all elements from the ArrayList.
Clone	Creates a shallow copy of the ArrayList.
Contains	Determines whether an element is in the ArrayList.
CopyTo(Array)	Copies the entire ArrayList to a compatible one-dimensional Array, starting at the beginning of the target array.
CopyTo(Array, Int32)	Copies the entire ArrayList to a compatible one-dimensional Array, starting at the specified index of the target array.
CopyTo(Int32, Array, Int32, Int32)	Copies a range of elements from the ArrayList to a compatible one-dimensional Array, starting at the specified index of the target array.
Equals(Object)	Determines whether the specified Object is equal to the current Object. (Inherited from Object.)
GetRange	Returns an ArrayList which represents a subset of the elements in the source ArrayList.
IndexOf(Object)	Searches for the specified Object and returns the zero-based index of the first occurrence within the entire ArrayList.
IndexOf(Object, Int32)	Searches for the specified Object and returns the zero-based index of the first occurrence within the range of elements in the ArrayList that extends from the specified index to the last element.
IndexOf(Object, Int32, Int32)	Searches for the specified Object and returns the zero-based index of the first occurrence within the range of elements in the ArrayList that starts at the specified index and contains the specified number of elements.
Insert	Inserts an element into the ArrayList at the specified index.
InsertRange	Inserts the elements of a collection into the ArrayList at the specified index.
LastIndexOf(Object)	Searches for the specified Object and returns the zero-based index of the last

occurrence within the entire ArrayList.

LastIndexOf(Object, Int32)	Searches for the specified Object and returns the zero-based index of the last occurrence within the range of elements in the ArrayList that extends from the first element to the specified index.
LastIndexOf(Object, Int32, Int32)	Searches for the specified Object and returns the zero-based index of the last occurrence within the range of elements in the ArrayList that contains the specified number of elements and ends at the specified index.
Remove	Removes the first occurrence of a specific object from the ArrayList.
RemoveAt	Removes the element at the specified index of the ArrayList.
RemoveRange	Removes a range of elements from the ArrayList.
Reverse()	Reverses the order of the elements in the entire ArrayList.
Reverse(Int32, Int32)	Reverses the order of the elements in the specified range.
Sort()	Sorts the elements in the entire ArrayList.
Sort(Int32, Int32)	Sorts the elements in a range of elements in ArrayList using the specified comparer.
ToArray()	Copies the elements of the ArrayList to a new Object array.
ToArray(Type)	Copies the elements of the ArrayList to a new array of the specified element type.
TrimToSize	Sets the capacity to the actual number of elements in the ArrayList.

Properties

Name	Description
Capacity	Gets or sets the number of elements that the ArrayList can contain.
Count	Gets the number of elements actually contained in the ArrayList.
IsFixedSize	Gets a value indicating whether the ArrayList has a fixed size.
IsReadOnly	Gets a value indicating whether the ArrayList is read-only.
IsSynchronized	Gets a value indicating whether access to the ArrayList is synchronized (thread safe).
Item	Gets or sets the element at the specified index.
SyncRoot	Gets an object that can be used to synchronize access to the ArrayList.

➤ **Stack**

The System.Collections.Stack class is a kind of collection that provides controlled access to its elements. A stack works on the principle of Last In First Out (LIFO), which means that the last item inserted into the stack will be the first item to be removed from it. Stacks and Queues are very common data structures in computer science and they are implemented in both hardware and software. The insertion of an item onto the stack is termed as a 'Push' while removing an item from the stack is called a 'Pop'. If the item is not removed but only read from the top of the stack, then this is called a 'Peek' operation. The System.Collections.Stack class provides the functionality of a Stack in the .Net environment. The Stack class can be instantiated in a manner similar to the one we used for the ArrayList. The three constructors for the Stack class are:

C# Programming Made Easy

Stack stack = new Stack();

The above (default) constructor will initialize a new empty stack. The following constructor call will initialize the stack with the supplied initial capacity:

Stack stack = new Stack(12);

While the following constructor will initialize the Stack with the supplied collection:

```
using System;
using System.Collections;
namespace CSharpSchool
{
        class Test
        {
                static void Main()
                {
                        Stack stack = new Stack();
                        stack.Push(2);
                        stack.Push(4);
                        stack.Push(6);
                        while(stack.Count != 0)
                        {
                                Console.WriteLine(stack.Pop());
                        }
                }
        }
}
```

Note that we have used a while() loop here to iterate through the elements of the stack. One thing to remember in the case of a stack is that the Pop() operation not only returns the element at the top of stack, but also removes the top element so the Count value will decrease with each Pop() operation. The output of the above program will be:

6
4
2

The other methods in the Stack class are very similar to those of an ArrayList except for the Peek() method. The Peek() method returns the top element of the stack without removing it. The following program demonstrates the use of the Peek() operation.

```
static void Main()
{
        Stack stack = new Stack();
        stack.Push(2);
        stack.Push(4);
        stack.Push(6);
    Console.WriteLine("The total number of elements on the stack
    before Peek() = {0}", stack.Count);
    Console.WriteLine("The top element of stack is {0}",
    stack.Peek());
    Console.WriteLine("The total number of elements on the stack
    after Peek() = {0}", stack.Count);
}
```

C# Programming Made Easy

The above program pushes three elements onto the stack and then peeks at the top element on the stack. The program prints the number of elements on the stack before and after the Peek() operation. The result of the program is:

The total number of elements on the stack before Peek() = 3
The top element of stack is 6
The total number of elements on the stack after Peek() = 3

The output of the program shows that Peek() does not affect the number of elements on the stack and does not remove the top element, contrary to the Pop() operation.

Methods

Name	Description
Clear	Removes all objects from the Stack.
Clone	Creates a shallow copy of the Stack.
Contains	Determines whether an element is in the Stack.
CopyTo	Copies the Stack to an existing one-dimensional Array, starting at the specified array index.
Equals(Object)	Determines whether the specified Object is equal to the current Object. (Inherited from Object.)
Peek	Returns the object at the top of the Stack without removing it.
Pop	Removes and returns the object at the top of the Stack.
Push	Inserts an object at the top of the Stack.
ToArray	Copies the Stack to a new array.
ToString	Returns a String that represents the current Object. (Inherited from Object.)

Properties

Name	Description
Count	Gets the number of elements contained in the Stack.
IsSynchronized	Gets a value indicating whether access to the Stack is synchronized (thread safe).
SyncRoot	Gets an object that can be used to synchronize access to the Stack.

➤ **Queue**

A Queue works on the principle of First In First Out (FIFO), which means that the first item inserted into the queue will be the first item removed from it. To 'Enqueue' an item is to insert it in the queue, and removal of an item from the queue is termed 'Dequeue'. Like a stack, there is also a Peek operation, where the item is not removed but only read from the front of the queue. The System.Collections.Queue class provides the functionality of queues in the .Net environment. The Queue's constructors are similar to those of the ArrayList and the Stack.

```
// an empty queue
Queue queue = new Queue();
```

```
// a queue with initial capacity 16
  Queue queue = new Queue(16);

// a queue containing elements from myCollection
Queue queue = new Queue(myCollection);
```

The following program demonstrates the use of Queues in C#.

```
static void Main()
{
        Queue queue = new Queue();
        queue.Enqueue(2);
        queue.Enqueue(4);
        queue.Enqueue(6);
        while(queue.Count != 0)
        {
                Console.WriteLine(queue.Dequeue());
        }
}
```

The program enqueues three elements into the Queue and then dequeues them using a while loop. The output of the program is:

```
2
4
6
```

The output shows that the queue removes items in the order they were inserted. The other methods of a Queue are very similar to those of the ArrayList and Stack classes.

Methods

Name	Description
Clear	Removes all objects from the Queue.
Clone	Creates a shallow copy of the Queue.
Contains	Determines whether an element is in the Queue.
CopyTo	Copies the Queue elements to an existing one-dimensional Array, starting at the specified array index.
Dequeue	Removes and returns the object at the beginning of the Queue.
Enqueue	Adds an object to the end of the Queue.
Equals(Object)	Determines whether the specified Object is equal to the current Object. (Inherited from Object.)
Peek	Returns the object at the beginning of the Queue without removing it.
ToArray	Copies the Queue elements to a new array.
ToString	Returns a String that represents the current Object. (Inherited from Object.)
TrimToSize	Sets the capacity to the actual number of elements in the Queue.

Properties

Name	Description
Count	Gets the number of elements contained in the Queue.
IsSynchronized	Gets a value indicating whether access to the Queue is synchronized (thread safe).
SyncRoot	Gets an object that can be used to synchronize access to the Queue.

➤ **Dictionaries**

Dictionaries are a kind of collection that store items in a key-value pair fashion. Each value in the collection is identified by its key. All the keys in the collection are unique and there can not be more than one key with the same name. This is similar to the English language dictionary like the Oxford Dictionary where each word (key) has its corresponding meaning (value). The two most common types of Dictionaries in the System.Collections namespace are the Hashtable and the SortedList.

➤ **Hashtable**

Hashtable stores items as key-value pairs. Each item (or value) in the hashtable is uniquely identified by its key. A hashtable stores the key and its value as an object type. Mostly the string class is used as the key in a hashtable, but you can use any other class as a key. However, before selecting a class for the key, be sure to override the Equals() and GetHashCode() methods that it inherit from the object class such that:

* Equals() checks for instance equality rather than the default reference equality.
* GetHashCode() returns the same integer for similar instances of the class.
* The values returned by GetHashCode() are evenly distributed between the MinValue and the MaxValue of the Integer type.

Constructing a Hashtable

The string and some of the other classes provided in the Base Class Library do consider these issues, and they are very suitable for usage as a key in hashtables or other dictionaries. There are many constructors available to instantiate a hashtable; some are:

```
Hashtable ht = new Hashtable();
```

Which is a default no argument constructor. A hashtable can also be constructed by passing in the initial capacity:

```
Hashtable ht = new Hashtable(20);
```

The Hashtable class also contains some other constructors which allow you to initialize the hashtable with some other collection or dictionary.

Adding items to a Hashtable

Once you have instantiated a hashtable object, then you can add items to it using its Add() method:

```
ht.Add("st01", "Faraz");
ht.Add("sci01", "Newton");
```

ht.Add("sci02", "Einstein");

Retrieving items from the Hashtable

Retrieving items from the Hashtable
Here we have inserted three items into the hashtable along with their keys. Any particular item can be retrieved using its key:

```
Console.WriteLine("Size of Hashtable is {0}", ht.Count);
Console.WriteLine("Element with key = st01 is {0}", ht["st01"]);
Console.WriteLine("Size of Hashtable is {0}", ht.Count);
```

Here we have used the indexer ([] operator) to retrieve the value from the hashtable. This way of retrieval does not remove the element from the hashtable but just returns the object with the specified key. Therefore, the size before and after the retrieval operation is always same (that is 3). The output of the code above is:

Size of Hashtable is 3
Element with key = st01 is Faraz
Size of Hashtable is 3

Removing a particular item

The elements of the hashtable can be removed by using the Remove() method which takes the key of the item to be removed as its argument.

```
static void Main()
{
        Hashtable ht =  new Hashtable(20);
        ht.Add("st01", "Faraz");
        ht.Add("sci01", "Newton");
        ht.Add("sci02", "Einstein");
        Console.WriteLine("Size of Hashtable is {0}", ht.Count);
        Console.WriteLine("Removing element with key = st01");
        ht.Remove("st01");
        Console.WriteLine("Size of Hashtable is {0}", ht.Count);
}
```

The output of the program is:

Size of Hashtable is 3
Removing element with key = st01
Size of Hashtable is 2

Getting the collection of keys and values

The collection of all the keys and values in a hashtable can be retrieved using the Keys and Values property, which return an ICollection containing all the keys and values respectively. The following program iterates through all the keys and values and prints them, using a foreach loop.

```
static void Main()
{
```

```
            Hashtable ht = new Hashtable(20);
            ht.Add("st01", "Faraz");
            ht.Add("sci01", "Newton");
            ht.Add("sci02", "Einstein");
            Console.WriteLine("Printing Keys...");
            foreach(string key in ht.Keys)
            {
                    Console.WriteLine(key);
            }
            Console.WriteLine("\nPrinting Values...");
            foreach(string Value in ht.Values)
            {
                    Console.WriteLine(Value);
            }
    }
```

The output of the program will be:

Printing Keys...
st01
sci02
sci01

Printing Values...
Faraz
Einstein
Newton

Checking the existence of a particular item in the hashtable

You can use the ContainsKey() and the ContainsValue() method to find out whether a particular item with the specified key and value exists in the hashtable or not. Both the methods return a boolean value.

```
        static void Main()
        {
                Hashtable ht = new Hashtable(20);
                ht.Add("st01", "Faraz");
                ht.Add("sci01", "Newton");
                ht.Add("sci02", "Einstein");
                Console.WriteLine(ht.ContainsKey("sci01"));
                Console.WriteLine(ht.ContainsKey("st00"));
                Console.WriteLine(ht.ContainsValue("Einstein"));
        }
```

The output is:

True
False
True

Indicating whether the elements in question exist in the dictionary (hashtable) or not.

Methods

Name	Description
Add	Adds an element with the specified key and value into the Hashtable.
Clear	Removes all elements from the Hashtable.
Clone	Creates a shallow copy of the Hashtable.
Contains	Determines whether the Hashtable contains a specific key.
ContainsKey	Determines whether the Hashtable contains a specific key.
ContainsValue	Determines whether the Hashtable contains a specific value.
CopyTo	Copies the Hashtable elements to a one-dimensional Array instance at the specified index.
Equals(Object)	Determines whether the specified Object is equal to the current Object. (Inherited from Object.)
KeyEquals	Compares a specific Object with a specific key in the Hashtable.
Remove	Removes the element with the specified key from the Hashtable.
ToString	Returns a String that represents the current Object. (Inherited from Object.)

Properties

Name	Description
Count	Gets the number of key/value pairs contained in the Hashtable.
IsFixedSize	Gets a value indicating whether the Hashtable has a fixed size.
IsReadOnly	Gets a value indicating whether the Hashtable is read-only.
IsSynchronized	Gets a value indicating whether access to the Hashtable is synchronized (thread safe).
Item	Gets or sets the value associated with the specified key.
Keys	Gets an ICollection containing the keys in the Hashtable.
SyncRoot	Gets an object that can be used to synchronize access to the Hashtable.
Values	Gets an ICollection containing the values in the Hashtable.

> ➢ **SortedList**

The sorted list class is similar to the Hashtable, the difference being that the items are sorted according to the key. One of the advantages of using a SortedList is that you can get the items in the collection using an integer index, just like you can with an array. In the case of SortedList, if you want to use your own class as a key then, in addition to the considerations described in Hashtable, you also need to make sure that your class implements the IComparable interface.

The IComparable interface has only one method int CompareTo(object obj)

This method takes the object type argument and returns an integer representing whether the supplied object is equal to, greater than or less than the current object.

* A return value of 0 indicates that this object is equal to the supplied obj.
* A return value greater than zero indicates that this object is greater than the supplied obj
* A return value less than zero indicates that this object is less than the supplied obj.

The string class and other primitive data types provide an implementation of this interface and hence can be used as keys in a SortedList directly.

The SortedList provides similar constructors as provided by the Hashtable and the simplest one is a zero argument constructor.

```
SortedList sl = new SortedList();
```

The following program demonstrates the use of a SortedList.

```
static void Main()
{
        SortedList sl = new SortedList();
        sl.Add(32, "Java");
        sl.Add(21, "C#");
        sl.Add(7, "VB.Net");
        sl.Add(49, "C++");
        Console.WriteLine("The items in the sorted order are...");
        Console.WriteLine("\t Key \t\t Value");
        Console.WriteLine("\t === \t\t =====");
        for(int i=0; i<sl.Count; i++)
        {
                Console.WriteLine("\t {0} \t\t {1}", sl.GetKey(i),
        sl.GetByIndex(i));
        }
}
```

The program stores the names of different programming languages (in string form) using integer keys. Then the for loop is used to retrieve the keys and values contained in the SortedList (sl). Since this is a sorted list, the items are internally stored in a sorted order and when we retrieve these names by the GetKey() or the GetByIndex() method, we get a sorted list of items. The output of the program will be:

The items in the sorted order are...
Key Value
=== =====
7 VB.Net
21 C#
32 Java
49 C++

Methods

Name	Description
Add	Adds an element with the specified key and value to a SortedList object.
Clear	Removes all elements from a SortedList object.
Clone	Creates a shallow copy of a SortedList object.

Contains	Determines whether a SortedList object contains a specific key.
ContainsKey	Determines whether a SortedList object contains a specific key.
ContainsValue	Determines whether a SortedList object contains a specific value.
CopyTo	Copies SortedList elements to a one-dimensional Array object, starting at the specified index in the array.
Equals(Object)	Determines whether the specified Object is equal to the current Object. (Inherited from Object.)
GetByIndex	Gets the value at the specified index of a SortedList object.
GetKey	Gets the key at the specified index of a SortedList object.
GetKeyList	Gets the keys in a SortedList object.
GetValueList	Gets the values in a SortedList object.
IndexOfKey	Returns the zero-based index of the specified key in a SortedList object.
IndexOfValue	Returns the zero-based index of the first occurrence of the specified value in a SortedList object.
Remove	Removes the element with the specified key from a SortedList object.
RemoveAt	Removes the element at the specified index of a SortedList object.
SetByIndex	Replaces the value at a specific index in a SortedList object.
ToString	Returns a String that represents the current Object. (Inherited from Object.)
TrimToSize	Sets the capacity to the actual number of elements in a SortedList object.

Properties

Name	Description
Capacity	Gets or sets the capacity of a SortedList object.
Count	Gets the number of elements contained in a SortedList object.
IsFixedSize	Gets a value indicating whether a SortedList object has a fixed size.
IsReadOnly	Gets a value indicating whether a SortedList object is read-only.
IsSynchronized	Gets a value indicating whether access to a SortedList object is synchronized (thread safe).
Item	Gets and sets the value associated with a specific key in a SortedList object.
Keys	Gets the keys in a SortedList object.
SyncRoot	Gets an object that can be used to synchronize access to a SortedList object.
Values	Gets the values in a SortedList object.

❖ Generics

Generics are the most highlighted addition to the C# language. Generics allow us to write general implementation of a type (class, structure, and interface), which is specialized by the compiler and runtime environment (CLR) based on the types that use it. Generics have been there in the programming world for a long time. In C++ they are called templates. Generics introduce a good amount of reuse in your programs reducing a lot of code.

➢ Why Generics?

I know the above text would be unable to clear the idea of generics till now. So let's investigate why in the world we need generics. In the current version (1.x) of C#, we write our ArrayList class as

```
class MyArrayList
{
        private object[] items;
        private int count=0;
        ...
        public void Add(object item)
        {
                items[count++] = item;
        }
        public object GetItem(int index)
        {
                return items[index];
        }
}
```

The problem with the class is that it is too general. You can add objects of any type and when we retrieve these objects we don't know the type of the object we are about to get and we need to cast it to what we expect!

```
MyArrayList list = new MyArrayList();
// Any type of items can be added
list.Add(5);
list.Add("C# Programming Language");
// Items retrieved would be of multiple types
int iValue = (int) list.GetItem(0);
string strValue = (string) list.GetItem(1);
```

One solutions is to write a specialized version of the type, for example

```
class MyIntArrayList
{
        private int[] items;
        private int count;
        ...
        public void Add(int item)
        {
                items[count] = item;
        }
        public int GetItem(int index)
        {
                return items[index];
```

```
       }
    }
```

and

```
    class MyStringArrayList
    {
            private string[] items;
            private int count;
            ...
            public void Add(string item)
            {
                    items[count] = item;
            }
            public string GetItem(int index)
            {
                    return items[index];
            }
    }
```

Now we can write the type safe code as

```
    // Integer ArrayList
    MyIntArrayList iList = new MyIntArrayList();
            // Only integers can be added
    iList.Add(5);
    iList.Add(7);
            // Only integers would be retrieved, no cast is required
    int iValue1 = iList.GetItem(0);
    int iValue2 = iList.GetItem(1);
    // String ArrayList
    MyIntArrayList strList = new MyStringArrayList();
            // Only strings can be added
    strList.Add("C# Programming Language");
            // Only strings would be retrieved, no cast is required
    string strValue = list.GetItem(0);
```

BUT indeed it is not a very smart solution and in many cases is not even possible. Can we (even imagine to) write the specialized classes for each and every type that might use our collection or algorithm? Definitely NO! What to do now? The answer is generics!

➢ **Generics and their implementation**

Now read the definition again, "Generics allow us to write general implementation of a type (class, structure, and interface) which is specialized by the compiler and runtime environment (CLR) based on the types that use it". Using generics we can write our Array List class as

```
using System;
// Defining a Generic Class
class MyArrayList<ItemType>
{
    private const int CAPACITY = 10;
    private ItemType[] items = new ItemType[CAPACITY];
    private int count = 0;
    public void Add(ItemType item)
        {
```

```
if (count < CAPACITY)
{
    items[count++] = item;
}
else
{
    throw new Exception("The list is full!");
}
}
    public ItemType GetItem(int index)
    {
if (index < count && index >= 0)
{
    return items[index];
}
else
{
    throw new Exception("Invalid index supplied");
}
}
}
```

These simple modifications to the original type do wonders! In the first line we declared that the class MyArrayList can be specialized for any data-type (either implicit or user defined) which would, later in the class, be referenced using the name ItemType class MyArrayList<ItemType>

Then we replaced the data type of items with ItemType. Note that ItemType is not a keyword but just an identifier, it is perfectly legal to use any identifier like 'a' or 'T' instead of 'ItemType'.

Now we can specialize MyArrayList for variety of types. For example, the code

```
MyArrayList<int> iList = new MyArrayList<int>();
```

will create an instance of MyArrayList class that accepts and return only integers or that has replaced ItemType in class definition with int. Now we can only add and retrieve integers from iList.

```
class Program
{
    static void Main(string[] args)
    {
        MyArrayList<int> iList = new MyArrayList<int>();
        iList.Add(4);      // only integers can be added
        iList.Add(102);
        iList.Add("some text");              // compile time error
        int iValue1 = iList.GetItem(0); // no cast required!!
        int iValue2 = iList.GetItem(1);
        string strValue = (string)iList.GetItem(1); // compile time error
        Console.ReadLine();
    }
}
```

Similarly for user defined type Person

```
static void Main(string[] args)
{
    MyArrayList<Person> pList = new MyArrayList<Person>();
```

```
pList.Add(new Person("He"));   // only Person type instances can be added
iList.Add("some text");        // compile time error
Person pValue = iList.GetItem(0);   // no cast required!!
}
```

Using multiple types in Generic type definition We can use more than one type in your generic type definition as

```
class MyDictionary<KeyType, ValueType>
{
    private KeyType[] keys;
    private ValueType[] values;
    private int count;
    ...
    public void Add(KeyType key, ValueType value)
    {
...
    }
}
```

Which can be instantiated and accessed as:

```
MyDictionary<int, string> dictionary = new MyDictionary<int, string>();
dictionary.Add(5, "Faraz");
```

➢ **Defining Constraints**

Some times your implementation requires that the type specializing your generic type has certain methods or properties. For example, let some where in our implementation we use

```
class MyGenericType<ItemType>
{
    private ItemType items;
    public void PerformSomeOperation()
    {
        foreach(object o in items)
        {
            // do something
        }
    }
}
```

Now if we instantiate the generic with integer type

```
MyGenericType<int> obj = new MyGenericType<int>();
```

And attempt to call the PerformSomeOperation() method, we apparently can't! As the integer type does not support foreach iterator or does not implement the IEnumerable() interface. So how can C# generics handle such situations? The answer is by using the constraints. For our MyGenericType, we can define a constraint as

```
class MyGenericType<ItemType> where ItemType : IEnumerable
{
    ...
}
```

Note that the C# compiler will raise an error if we do not provide the above mentioned constraints as not all classes implements the IEnumerable interface. Now MyGenericType can be instantiated only for those types that implement the IEnumerable interface

MyGenericType<ArrayList> obj = new MyGenericType<ArrayList>();
MyGenericType<int> obj1 = new MyGenericType<int>(); // compile time error

➤ **Types of Constraints**

There are five types of constraints that we can apply when defining a generic type in .Net

Constraint	Description
where T : struct	The type T must be a structure (value type)
where T : class	The type T must be a class (reference type)
where T : new	The type T must have a no-argument constructor
where T :	The type T must either be the specified class or its sub-class
where T :	The type T must either be the specified interface (or its sub-interface) or the class implementing the interface

Multiple Constraints

You may define multiple constraints with generics separating each of them with a comma like

```
class MyDictionary<KeyType, ValueType>
    where KeyType : IEnumerable, new()
{
    ...
}
```

It says that the class specializing this generic must implement the IEnumerable interface (can be iterated through the foreach loop) and contains the no-argument constructor.

If your generic has more than one type, you can define separate constraints for both types starting each type constraint with the 'where' clause

```
class MyDictionary<KeyType, ValueType>
    where KeyType : IComparable
    where ValueType : System.Runtime.Serialization.ISerializable
{
    ...
}
```

➤ **Generic Methods**

Just as we can use the generics with types; we can also use generics to define method signatures. In C#, a method may have generic parameter types as well as a generic return type. Some applications may need this feature in order to avoid the unnecessary method overloading. For example consider the following generic method

```
public T Perform<T> (T val, int num)
{
```

```
    return val;
}
```

When using the above method, one has to specialize it with a type which will be used as one of its parameter type as well as its return type. For example, when we want to specialize this method with the string type, we used the following method invocation syntax

```
MyType obj = new MyType();
string strVal = obj.Perform<string>("faraz", 1);
```

Note that using generic methods is exactly similar to using generic types. We can also define constraints with generic methods as we used with the generic types.

> **Inside the generics implementation**

In C++ templates and proposed generics in Java, generics are resolved at compile time and the runtime environment (JVM in case of Java) is not even aware of any template or generic. While in case of C#, generics are declared and type checked at compile time while instantiated at runtime just like any other object. Also because of the boxing/unboxing feature of C#, generics can be applied to all the types including the implicit data types. Finally, since C# generics preserve types at runtime, they can be recognized using reflection.

❖ Generics List

You have questions about the **List** collection in the .NET Framework, which is located in the System.Collections.Generic namespace. You want to see examples of using List and also explore some of the many useful methods it provides, making it an ideal type for dynamically adding data. This document has lots of tips and resources on the List constructed type, with examples using the C# programming language.

--- Key points: ---
Lists are dynamic arrays in the C# language.
They can grow as needed when you add elements.
They are called generic collections and constructed types.
You need to use < and > in the List declaration.

> **Adding values**

Here we see how to declare a new List of int values and add integers to it. This example shows how you can create a new List of unspecified size, and add four prime numbers to it. Importantly, the angle brackets are part of the declaration type, not conditional operators that mean less or more than. They are treated differently in the language.

~~~ **Program that adds elements to List (C#)** ~~~

```
using System.Collections.Generic;

class Program
{
```

```
static void Main()
{
    List<int> list = new List<int>();
    list.Add(2);
    list.Add(3);
    list.Add(5);
    list.Add(7);
}
}
```

➢ **Adding objects.**

The above example shows how you can add a primitive type such as integer to a List collection, but the List collection can receive reference types and object instances. There is more information on adding objects with the Add method on this site.
You want to add an element that is either a value type or a reference type to your **List instance** in the C# language. The Add instance method on the List type has internal logic that allows you to add elements to the end of the collection quickly. Here we look at how you can invoke the Add method on the List constructed type in the C# programming language to add an element type to the end of a List.

✓ **Using Add method**

First, here we declare a new List with an integer (Int32) type parameter and use the **Add** method four times. This example shows how you can create a new List of unspecified size, and add four prime numbers to it. Importantly, the angle brackets are part of the declaration type, not conditional operators that mean less or more than. They are treated differently in the language.
~~~ Program that uses Add method (C#) ~~~

```
using System.Collections.Generic;

class Program
{
    static void Main()
    {
        // Add first four numbers to the List.
        List<int> primes = new List<int>();
        primes.Add(2);
        primes.Add(3);
        primes.Add(5);
        primes.Add(7);
    }
}
```

Program result. When you execute the above program, the List instance called 'primes' will contain four integers in its internal data structure. The integers 2, 3, 5 and 7 will be stored in that order in the List's internal array. Whenever you loop over the List's contents, the integers will be accessed in that order.

Here we declare a custom **class**, and then add instances of it to a new List. The type in between the angle brackets is the name of the new class Test. This means the List will only contain Test objects. Because the Test type is a reference type, the List in the example will store reference values to the objects allocated as Test objects on the managed heap.

--- Program that adds objects to List (C#) ---

```
using System.Collections.Generic;

class Program
{
    static void Main()
    {
        // Add three objects to a List.
        List<Test> list = new List<Test>();
        list.Add(new Test(1, 2));
        list.Add(new Test(3, 4));
        list.Add(new Test(5, 6));
    }

    class Test
    {
        int _a;
        int _b;
        public Test(int a, int b)
        {
            _a = a;
            _b = b;
        }
    };
}
```

Description. The above example will allocate an object containing an internal array of Test object references. These object references do not contain the integer fields on the Test class inline; instead, the references contain the storage location of the Test class instance on the managed heap.

➢ **Loops**

Here we see how you can loop through your List with for and foreach loops. This is a very common operation when using List. The syntax is the same as that for an array, except your use

Count, not Length for the upper bound. You can also loop backwards through your List by reversing the for loop iteration variables. Start with list.Count - 1, and proceed decrementing to >= 0.

~~~ Program that loops through List (C#) ~~~

```
using System;
using System.Collections.Generic;

class Program
{
    static void Main()
    {
        List<int> list = new List<int>();
        list.Add(2);
        list.Add(3);
        list.Add(7);

        foreach (int prime in list) // Loop through List with foreach
        {
            Console.WriteLine(prime);
        }

        for (int i = 0; i < list.Count; i++) // Loop through List with for
        {
            Console.WriteLine(list[i]);
        }
    }
}
```

~~~ Output of the program ~~~
   (Repeated twice)
2
3
7

➤ **Counting elements**

To get the number of elements in your List, access the Count property. This is fast to access, if you avoid the Count() extension method. Count is equal to Length on arrays. See the section "Clearing List" for an example on using the Count property.

➤ **Clearing List—setting to null**

Here we see how to use the Clear method, along with the Count property, to erase all the elements in your List. Before Clear is called, this List has 3 elements; after Clear is called, it has 0

C# Programming Made Easy

elements. Alternatively, you can assign the List to null instead of calling Clear, with similar performance. However, after assigning to null, you must call the constructor again.

=== Program that counts List (C#) ===

```
using System;
using System.Collections.Generic;

class Program
{
    static void Main()
    {
        List<bool> list = new List<bool>();
        list.Add(true);
        list.Add(false);
        list.Add(true);
        Console.WriteLine(list.Count); // 3

        list.Clear();
        Console.WriteLine(list.Count); // 0
    }
}
```

=== Output of the program ===

```
3
0
```

> **Finding elements**

Here we an example of how you can test each element in your List for a certain value. This shows the foreach loop, which tests to see if 3 is in the List of prime numbers. Note that more advanced List methods are available to find matches in the List, but they often aren't any better than this loop. They can sometimes result in shorter code.

~~~ Program that uses foreach on List (C#) ~~~

```
using System;
using System.Collections.Generic;

class Program
{
    static void Main()
    {
        // New list for example
        List<int> primes = new List<int>(new int[] { 2, 3, 5 });
```

```
// See if List contains 3
foreach (int number in primes)
{
    if (number == 3) // Will match once
    {
        Console.WriteLine("Contains 3");
    }
}
}
}
```

~~~ **Output of the program** ~~~

Contains 3

How can you locate an element in your List collection using methods? You can **find elements** in your List using the advanced methods that take delegate methods in the C# programming language. These methods enhance the clarity and maintainability of your code, although they can be exchanged with loops. In this example set, we demonstrate the finding and searching methods, beginning with Find and moving on to Exists and IndexOf.

➢ **Getting element with Find**

Instead of using a foreach loop with an if statement, you can use the **Find** instance method on List. Here we see that it also accepts a Predicate, which you can specify as a lambda expression. It returns the first match.

--- **Program that uses Find method on List (C#)** ---

```
using System;
using System.Collections.Generic;

class Program
{
    static void Main()
    {
        List<int> list = new List<int>(new int[] { 19, 23, 29 });

        // Finds first element greater than 20
        int result = list.Find(item => item > 20);

        Console.WriteLine(result);
    }
}
```

23

Description. This code loops through each int value in the List, starting at the beginning, and tests each one to see if it is greater than 20. The first one that is, 23, is returned. The parameter to the Find method is a lambda expression that is considered a Predicate instance. Please see the article on the Predicate type for more specific examples.

> **Using Exists**

Here we see the **Exists method** on List, which is an instance method that returns true or false depending on whether any element matches the Predicate parameter. The Predicate is a method that returns true or false when passed each element.

```
using System;
using System.Collections.Generic;

class Program
{
    static void Main()
    {
        List<int> list = new List<int>();
        list.Add(7);
        list.Add(11);
        list.Add(13);

        // See if any elements with values greater than 10 exist
        bool exists = list.Exists(element => element > 10);
        Console.WriteLine(exists);

        // Check for numbers less than 7
        exists = list.Exists(element => element < 7);
        Console.WriteLine(exists);
    }
}
```

True
False

Description. The example for Exists above tests first to see if any element in the List exists that has a value greater than 10, which returns true. Then it tests for values less than 7, which returns false. You can also see the Find method above.

➢ **Using IndexOf**

Here we see the **IndexOf** instance method in List, which has two overloads and works the same way as string IndexOf. It accepts the value you want to find as the first parameter, and then returns the location of the value in the array.

--- Program that uses IndexOf method on List (C#) ---

```
using System;
using System.Collections.Generic;

class Program
{
    static void Main()
    {
        List<int> primes = new List<int>(new int[] { 19, 23, 29 });

        int index = primes.IndexOf(23); // Exists in List
        Console.WriteLine(index);

        index = primes.IndexOf(10); // Doesn't exist in List
        Console.WriteLine(index);
    }
}
```

--- Output of the program ---

```
1
-1
```

Description. When using IndexOf, you must always test for -1, or you will get exceptions that you will have to deal with elsewhere. Note that you can also use LastIndexOf to search in the reverse order. It also has overloads. There is no IndexOfAny method, as the string class has.

➢ **Understanding FindAll**

The **FindAll** method on List, which is an instance method that returns a new List with the same element type, is also available. If you want to find all the matching elements based on a Predicate, this is useful.

➢ **Using capacity**

You can use the Capacity property on List, or pass an integer into the constructor, to improve allocation performance when using List. The author's research shows that capacity can improve performance by nearly two times for adding elements. Note however that this is not usually a performance bottleneck in programs that access data.

➢ **Using BinarySearch**

You can use the binary search algorithm on List with the instance BinarySearch method. Binary search uses guesses to find the correct element much faster than linear searching. It is often much slower than Dictionary.

You are evaluating the **BinarySearch method** on List or arrays, and want data on whether it can improve your program. You have a variable number of elements in your collection. Binary search is an amazing algorithm that 'hones' in on values in sorted collections. It has O(log n) complexity, making it more efficient than others in the C# language.

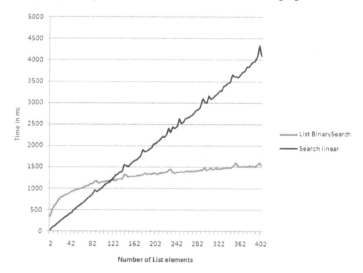

First, here we look at an example program that uses the BinarySearch instance method on the List type. You must pass this method a value of the type used in the List. Normally, programs use strings, so we use that type here.

=== Program that uses BinarySearch (C#) ===

```
using System;
using System.Collections.Generic;

class Program
```

```
{
  static void Main()
  {
    List<string> l = new List<string>();
    l.Add("acorn");     // 0
    l.Add("apple");     // 1
    l.Add("banana");    // 2
    l.Add("cantaloupe"); // 3
    l.Add("lettuce");   // 4
    l.Add("onion");     // 5
    l.Add("peach");     // 6
    l.Add("pepper");    // 7
    l.Add("squash");    // 8
    l.Add("tangerine"); // 9

    // This returns the index of "peach".
    int i = l.BinarySearch("peach");
    Console.WriteLine(i);

    // This returns the index of "banana".
    i = l.BinarySearch("banana");
    Console.WriteLine(i);

    // This returns the index of "apple".
    i = l.BinarySearch("apple");
    Console.WriteLine(i);
  }
}
```

=== Output of the program ===

6
2
1

Description. Three values are looked up. The locations of "peach", "banana", and "apple" are looked up in the List. Note that the List is in alphabetical order. BinarySearch won't work if your List or array is not already sorted. It doesn't matter if you use numeric, alphanumeric, or ASCII sorting.

➢ **Using AddRange and InsertRange**

You can use AddRange and InsertRange to add or insert collections of elements into your existing List. This can make your code simpler. See an example of these methods on this site.

✓ Using AddRange

C# Programming Made Easy

Here we look at the AddRange instance method from the base class library in the C# language on List. This example show you can add a range at the end of the List using the AddRange method. The term 'range' simply means an IEnumerable collection, which includes List, arrays, and others.

=== **Program that uses AddRange (C#) ===**

```
using System;
using System.Collections.Generic;

class Program
{
    static void Main()
    {
        List<int> a = new List<int>();
        a.Add(1);
        a.Add(2);
        a.Add(5);
        a.Add(6);

        // Contains:
        // 1
        // 2
        // 5
        // 6

        int[] b = new int[3];
        b[0] = 7;
        b[1] = 6;
        b[2] = 7;

        a.AddRange(b);

        // Contains:
        // 1
        // 2
        // 5
        // 6
        // 7 [added]
        // 6 [added]
        // 7 [added]
        foreach (int i in a)
        {
            Console.WriteLine(i);
        }
    }
}
```

}

=== Output of the program ===

1
2
5
6
7
6
7

Above, we see a new List created, and four ints added to it. Then, an array of three elements of the same numeric type is initialized. We then call AddRange as an instance method on List. It receives the array.

The end result of the above program is that it displays seven integers, which are the union of the List itself and the array we added with AddRange.

✓ Using InsertRange

First, the InsertRange is closely related to the AddRange method, which allows you to add an array or other collection on the end of a List. InsertRange, as shown below, is exactly the same except that it can insert the IEnumerable range in between existing elements, or at the very start.

=== Program that uses InsertRange (C#) ===

```
using System;
using System.Collections.Generic;

class Program
{
    static void Main()
    {
        List<int> a = new List<int>();
        a.Add(1);
        a.Add(2);
        a.Add(5);
        a.Add(6);

        // Contains:
        // 1
        // 2
        // 5
        // 6
```

```
int[] b = new int[3];
b[0] = 7;
b[1] = 6;
b[2] = 7;

a.InsertRange(1, b);

// Contains:
// 1
// 7 [inserted]
// 6 [inserted]
// 7 [inserted]
// 2
// 5
// 6
foreach (int i in a)
{
   Console.WriteLine(i);
}
   }
}
```

=== **Output of the program** ===

```
1
7
6
7
2
5
6
```

➢ **Using ForEach method**

Sometimes you may not want to write a regular foreach loop, which makes ForEach useful. This accepts an Action, which is a void delegate method. Be very cautious when you use Predicates and Actions, because they can decrease the readability of your code.

➢ **Using Join—string List**

Here we see how you can use string.Join on a List of strings. This is useful when you need to turn several strings into one comma-delimited string. It requires the ToArray instance method on List. The biggest advantage of Join here is that no trailing comma is present on the resulting string, which would be present in a loop where each string is appended.

=== Program that joins List (C#) ===

```
using System;
using System.Collections.Generic;

class Program
{
    static void Main()
    {
        // List of cities we need to join
        List<string> cities = new List<string>();
        cities.Add("New York");
        cities.Add("Mumbai");
        cities.Add("Berlin");
        cities.Add("Istanbul");

        // Join strings into one CSV line
        string line = string.Join(",", cities.ToArray());
        Console.WriteLine(line);
    }
}
```

=== Output of the program ===

New York,Mumbai,Berlin,Istanbul

➤ Getting List from Keys in Dictionary

Here we see how you can use the List constructor to get a List of keys in your Dictionary collection. This gives you a simple way to iterate over Dictionary keys, or store them elsewhere. The Keys instance property accessor on Dictionary returns an enumerable collection of keys, which can be passed to the List constructor as a parameter.

::: Program that converts Keys (C#) :::

```
using System;
using System.Collections.Generic;

class Program
{
    static void Main()
    {
        // Populate example Dictionary
        var dict = new Dictionary<int, bool>();
        dict.Add(3, true);
        dict.Add(5, false);
```

```
// Get a List of all the Keys
List<int> keys = new List<int>(dict.Keys);
foreach (int key in keys)
{
    Console.WriteLine(key);
}
  }
}
```

::: Output of the program :::

3, 5

➢ **Inserting elements**

Here we see how you can insert an element into your List at any position. The string "dalmation" is inserted into index 1, which makes it become the second element in the List. Note that if you have to Insert elements extensively, you should consider the Queue and LinkedList collections for better performance. Additionally, a Queue may provide clearer usage of the collection in your code.

~~~ Program that inserts into List (C#) ~~~

```
using System;
using System.Collections.Generic;

class Program
{
    static void Main()
    {
        List<string> dogs = new List<string>(); // Example List

        dogs.Add("spaniel");      // Contains: spaniel
        dogs.Add("beagle");       // Contains: spaniel, beagle
        dogs.Insert(1, "dalmation"); // Contains: spaniel, dalmation, beagle

        foreach (string dog in dogs) // Display for verification
        {
            Console.WriteLine(dog);
        }
    }
}
```

~~~ Output of the program ~~~

spaniel

dalmation
beagle

➤ Removing elements

The removal methods on List are covered in depth in another article on this site. It contains examples for Remove, RemoveAt, RemoveAll, and RemoveRange, along with the author's notes.
You are using the **List collection** in the C# programming language and need to remove certain elements. These can be at certain indexes, can have certain values, or match conditions. Here we see several examples of List.Remove methods in System.Collections.Generic, and also review resources.

First, here we see how you can **Remove**, erase elements from your List. You can do this based on the element value you want to remove, or based on the index. This is not equivalent to assigning an element to null.

=== Program that uses Remove method (C#) ===

```
using System;
using System.Collections.Generic;

class Program
{
    static void Main()
    {
        List<string> dogs = new List<string>();
        dogs.Add("maltese");    // Contains maltese
        dogs.Add("otterhound"); // maltese, otterhound
        dogs.Add("rottweiler"); // maltese, otterhound, rottweiler
        dogs.Add("bulldog");    // ... rottweiler, bulldog
        dogs.Add("whippet");    // .... rottweiler, bulldog, whippet

        dogs.Remove("bulldog"); // Remove bulldog

        foreach (string dog in dogs)
        {
            Console.WriteLine(dog);
        }
```

```
// Contains: maltese, otterhound, rottweiler, whippet

dogs.RemoveAt(1); // Remove second dog

        foreach (string dog in dogs)
        {
            Console.WriteLine(dog);
        }
        // Contains: maltese, rottweiler, whippet
    }
}
```

=== **Output of the program** ===

maltese
otterhound
rottweiler
whippet

maltese
rottweiler
whippet

Description. This example shows Remove and RemoveAt. It removes the element with the value "bulldog", which erases the fourth element from the dogs List. It then removes the element with index 1, which is the second dog, "otterhound".

✓ **Removing all except last elements**

Here we see the **RemoveRange** method, which can remove elements in a certain series of indexes. One of the most useful ways to use call this method is to remove the first N or last N elements at once. Here we remove all elements except the last two. The code is robust because it uses Math.Max to avoid negative parameters.

=== **Program that uses RemoveRange method (C#)** ===

```
using System;
using System.Collections.Generic;

class Program
{
    static void Main()
    {
        List<int> list = new List<int>();
        list.Add(1);
        list.Add(2);
```

```
list.Add(3);
list.Add(4);
list.Add(5);

// Remove all except last 2
int remove = Math.Max(0, list.Count - 2);
list.RemoveRange(0, remove);

foreach (int i in list)
{
    Console.Write(i);
}
    }
}
```

=== **Output of the program** ===

45

✓ Removing first elements

Another useful way to call **RemoveRange** is to remove the first N elements in your List. We also use Math.Min here to avoid arguments that are too large and would raise an exception.

=== **Program that uses RemoveRange on first elements (C#)** ===

```
using System;
using System.Collections.Generic;

class Program
{
    static void Main()
    {
        List<int> list = new List<int>();
        list.Add(1);
        list.Add(2);
        list.Add(3);
        list.Add(4);
        list.Add(5);

        // Remove first 2 elements
        int remove = Math.Min(list.Count, 2);
        list.RemoveRange(0, remove);

        foreach (int i in list)
        {
```

```
    Console.Write(i);
   }
  }
}
```

=== Output of the program ===

345

➢ Sorting and reversing

You can use the powerful Sort and Reverse methods in your List collection. These allow you to order your List in ascending or descending order. Additionally, you can use Reverse even when your List is not presorted. There is more information on these topics, as well as sorting your List with LINQ on a property on this site.

You are using the List constructed type in your program, and need to sort its contents in ascending or descending order, or by a property on the objects. The **Sort method** is ideal for some requirements, but you can use LINQ for a simple way to sort elements by properties. Here we look at how you can use the parameterless Sort instance method on List, and also the Reverse method and LINQ query expressions with List in the C# programming language.

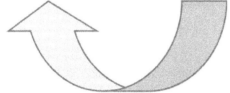

✓ Sorting List

Here we see how you can use the instance Sort method on your List to alphabetize its strings from A - Z. You could also specify a comparison function, or use the LINQ orderby keyword instead. This program will populate the List with three strings, and then sort them alphabetically. You can use the same method for integral types.

=== Program that uses Sort (C#) ===

```
using System;
using System.Collections.Generic;

class Program
{
    static void Main()
    {
        List<string> list = new List<string>();
        list.Add("tuna");
```

```
list.Add("velvetfish");
list.Add("angler");

// Sort fish alphabetically, in ascending order (A - Z)
list.Sort();

foreach (string value in list)
{
   Console.WriteLine(value);
}
}
}
```

=== Output of the program ===

angler
tuna
velvetfish

Note on sorting. You can combine the Sort method with the Reverse method to get a reverse sorted collection. Please see the next example for details. Sort works with all value types and classes that implement the CompareTo method.

✓ **Reversing List**

Here we see how you can **reverse** the order of the element collection in your List. You can use this method on an unsorted List, or you can combine this with an ascending sorting method to get a descending sort. This means you can change the ordering from A - Z to Z - A, which can be very useful.

=== Program that uses Reverse (C#) ===

```
using System;
using System.Collections.Generic;

class Program
{
   static void Main()
   {
      List<string> list = new List<string>();
      list.Add("anchovy");
      list.Add("barracuda");
      list.Add("bass");
      list.Add("viperfish");

      // Reverse List in-place, no new variables required
```

```
    list.Reverse();

    foreach (string value in list)
    {
        Console.WriteLine(value);
    }
  }
}
```

=== Output of the program ===

viperfish
bass
barracuda
anchovy

✓ **Sorting on property**

Here we see how you can use the LINQ **orderby** keyword to sort a List by any property. This makes it simple to sort based on string length, or a property value in any object type. LINQ works on IEnumerable collections, which include List, making this technique very useful in some programs.

=== **Program that Sorts with LINQ (C#)** ===

```
using System;
using System.Collections.Generic;
using System.Linq;

class Program
{
    static void Main()
    {
        List<string> list = new List<string>();
        list.Add("mississippi"); // Longest
        list.Add("indus");
        list.Add("danube");
        list.Add("nile"); // Shortest

        var lengths = from element in list
                orderby element.Length
                select element;

        foreach (string value in lengths)
        {
            Console.WriteLine(value);
```

```
      }
    }
}
```

=== Output of the program ===

nile
indus
danube
Mississippi

➢ **Converting List to array**

You can convert your List to an array of the same type using the instance method ToArray. There are examples of this conversion, and the opposite, on this site.

You have to **convert** your List to an array, or the opposite. This is needed in many programs and it is important to have it handy. Make sure your method works well and look at it in the debugger. Here we look at some examples of converting arrays and Lists in the C# programming language.

Here we look at how you can convert your List to an array, using the string element type. There are two parts to this example. In part A, the example creates a new List and populates it with some strings. The List is a constructed type and can only hold strings. Next, in part B it uses ToArray on the List.

=== Program that uses ToArray (C#) ===

```
using System;
using System.Collections.Generic;
using System.Linq;
using System.Text;

class Program
{
    static void Main()
    {
        // A.
        // New list here.
```

```
List<string> l = new List<string>();
l.Add("one");
l.Add("two");
l.Add("three");
l.Add("four");
l.Add("five");

    // B.
    string[] s = l.ToArray();
  }
}
```

➤ **Converting array to List**

Here we look at how you can convert an array of any number of elements to a List that has the same type of elements. There are three parts to this example. First, in part 1 it initializes a new string[] array containing 5 strings. Next, in part 2A it converts the array to a to List with the new List constructor. In part 2B, the example converts the array to a List with the ToList() parameterless instance method.

=== Program that uses List constructor and ToList (C#) ===

```
using System;
using System.Collections.Generic;
using System.Linq;
using System.Text;

class Program
{
  static void Main()
  {
    // 1.
    // String array
    string[] s = new string[]
    {
      "one",
      "two",
      "three",
      "four",
      "five"
    };
    // 2A.
    // Convert with new List constructor.
    List<string> l = new List<string>(s);

    // 2B.
```

```
        List<string> l2 = s.ToList();
    }
}
```

You have a List collection and want to copy the elements in it to a simple array. The List type's **CopyTo** instance method provides a way to do this in one declarative function call. When using the CopyTo method, you must make sure the array is properly allocated, as we show in this article.

➢ **Using List CopyTo method**

To start, this program creates a List of int values with three elements in it: the values 5, 6, and 7. Next, an int[] array is allocated; it has a length equal to the Count of the List. Third, the CopyTo method is invoked upon the list variable; the parameter is the array reference we just allocated. Finally, we prove that the array now contains all the elements of the originating List.

::: **Program that uses CopyTo on List (C#)** :::

```
using System;
using System.Collections.Generic;

class Program
{
    static void Main()
    {
        // Create a list with three elements.
        var list = new List<int>() { 5, 6, 7 };

        // Create an array with length of three.
        int[] array = new int[list.Count];

        // Copy the list to the array.
        list.CopyTo(array);

        // Display.
        Console.WriteLine(array[0]);
        Console.WriteLine(array[1]);
        Console.WriteLine(array[2]);
    }
}
```

::: **Output of the program** :::

```
5
6
7
```

➢ **Getting range of elements**

Here we see how you can get a range of elements in your List collection using the GetRange instance method. This is similar to the Take and Skip methods from LINQ, but has different syntax.

--- Program that gets ranges from List (C#) ---

```
using System;
using System.Collections.Generic;

class Program
{
    static void Main()
    {
        List<string> rivers = new List<string>(new string[]
        {
            "nile",
            "amazon",    // River 2
            "yangtze",   // River 3
            "mississippi",
            "yellow"
        });

        // Get rivers 2 through 3
        List<string> range = rivers.GetRange(1, 2);
        foreach (string river in range)
        {
            Console.WriteLine(river);
        }
    }
}
```

--- Output of the program ---

amazon
Yangtze

➢ **Testing Lists for equality**

Sometimes you may need to test two Lists for equality, even when their elements are unordered. You can do this by sorting both of them and then comparing, or by using a custom List equality method. This site contains an example of a method that tests lists for equality in an unordered way.

You want to determine if two Lists or arrays have the **same element values**, regardless of order. There are many possible approaches, but you want the simplest. Here we look at some research and develop a solution to test for List equality, using the C# programming language.

List 1 contents: 1, 2, 4
List 2 contents: 2, 1, 4
Equal?:   True

List 1 contents: 5, 4, 6
List 2 contents: 6, 5, 4
Equal?:   True

List 1 contents: 1, 2, 4
List 2 contents: 1, 4
Equal?:   False

List 1 contents: 1, 5
List 2 contents: 2, 5
Equal?:   False

List 1 contents: 1, 2
List 2 contents: 1, 2
Equal?:   True

Before developing the solution, I researched on Google and found a variety of approaches. One solution copies both Lists to arrays, sorts them, and then loops over the elements. The best versions use Dictionary and compare the frequencies. Here we see a generic method in C#, meaning it receives parameters of a caller-specified type. The syntax uses the angle brackets, < and >.

~~~ Program that tests List equality (C#) ~~~

```
using System;
using System.Collections.Generic;

class Program
{
    static void Main()
    {
        List<int> la = new List<int>() { 1, 0, 4, 200, -40 };
        List<int> lb = new List<int>() { -40, 200, 4, 1, 0 };
        List<int> lc = new List<int>() { 3, 5, 4, 9, 11 };
        List<int> ld = new List<int>() { 6, 6, 100 };
        List<int> le = new List<int>() { 6, 100, 100 };
        Console.WriteLine(UnorderedEqual(la, lb)); // true
        Console.WriteLine(UnorderedEqual(la, lc)); // false
        Console.WriteLine(UnorderedEqual(lc, ld)); // false
```

```
Console.WriteLine(UnorderedEqual(ld, le)); // false

int[] a1 = new int[] { 1, 2, 5 };
int[] a2 = new int[] { 2, 5, 1 };
int[] a3 = new int[] { 1, 1, 3 };
int[] a4 = new int[] { 3, 3, 1 };
Console.WriteLine(UnorderedEqual(a1, a2)); // true
Console.WriteLine(UnorderedEqual(a1, a3)); // false
Console.WriteLine(UnorderedEqual(a3, a4)); // false
}

static bool UnorderedEqual<T>(ICollection<T> a, ICollection<T> b)
{
    // 1
    // Require that the counts are equal
    if (a.Count != b.Count)
    {
        return false;
    }
    // 2
    // Initialize new Dictionary of the type
    Dictionary<T, int> d = new Dictionary<T, int>();
    // 3
    // Add each key's frequency from collection A to the Dictionary
    foreach (T item in a)
    {
        int c;
        if (d.TryGetValue(item, out c))
        {
            d[item] = c + 1;
        }
        else
        {
            d.Add(item, 1);
        }
    }
    // 4
    // Add each key's frequency from collection B to the Dictionary
    // Return early if we detect a mismatch
    foreach (T item in b)
    {
        int c;
        if (d.TryGetValue(item, out c))
        {
            if (c == 0)
            {
```

```
      return false;
    }
    else
    {
      d[item] = c - 1;
    }
  }
  else
  {
    // Not in dictionary
    return false;
  }
}
// 5
// Verify that all frequencies are zero
foreach (int v in d.Values)
{
  if (v != 0)
  {
    return false;
  }
}
// 6
// We know the collections are equal
return true;
  }
}
```

➢ **Using List with structs**

When using List, you can improve performance and reduce memory usage with structs instead of classes. A List of structs is allocated in contiguous memory, unlike a List of classes. This is an advanced optimization. Note that in many cases using structs will actually decrease the performance when they are used as parameters in methods such as those on the List type.

➢ **Using var keyword**

Here we see how you can use List collections with the var keyword. This can greatly shorten your lines of code, which sometimes improves readability. The var keyword has no effect on performance, only readability for programmers.

~~~ Program that uses var with List (C#) ~~~

```
using System.Collections.Generic;

class Program
```

```
{
  static void Main()
  {
    var list1 = new List<int>();      // <- var keyword used
    List<int> list2 = new List<int>(); // <- Is equivalent to
  }
}
```

❖ Generics Stack

Stack<T> Class represents a variable size last-in-first-out (LIFO) collection of instances of the same arbitrary type. Stack<T> is implemented as an array.

The capacity of a Stack<T> is the number of elements the Stack<T> can hold. As elements are added to a Stack<T>, the capacity is automatically increased as required by reallocating the internal array. The capacity can be decreased by calling TrimExcess.

If Count is less than the capacity of the stack, Push is an O(1) operation. If the capacity needs to be increased to accommodate the new element, Push becomes an O(n) operation, where n is Count. Pop is an O(1) operation.

Stack<T> accepts null as a valid value for reference types and allows duplicate elements.

Example

The following code example demonstrates several methods of the Stack<T> generic class. The code example creates a stack of strings with default capacity and uses the Push method to push five strings onto the stack. The elements of the stack are enumerated, which does not change the state of the stack. The Pop method is used to pop the first string off the stack. The Peek method is used to look at the next item on the stack, and then the Pop method is used to pop it off.

The ToArray method is used to create an array and copy the stack elements to it, then the array is passed to the Stack<T> constructor that takes IEnumerable<T>, creating a copy of the stack with the order of the elements reversed. The elements of the copy are displayed.

An array twice the size of the stack is created, and the CopyTo method is used to copy the array elements beginning at the middle of the array. The Stack<T> constructor is used again to create a copy of the stack with the order of elements reversed; thus, the three null elements are at the end.

The Contains method is used to show that the string "four" is in the first copy of the stack, after which the Clear method clears the copy and the Count property shows that the stack is empty.

using System;

```
using System.Collections.Generic;

class Example
{
  public static void Main()
  {
    Stack<string> numbers = new Stack<string>();
    numbers.Push("one");
    numbers.Push("two");
    numbers.Push("three");
    numbers.Push("four");
    numbers.Push("five");

    // A stack can be enumerated without disturbing its contents.
    foreach( string number in numbers )
    {
      Console.WriteLine(number);
    }

    Console.WriteLine("\nPopping '{0}'", numbers.Pop());
    Console.WriteLine("Peek at next item to destack: {0}",
      numbers.Peek());
    Console.WriteLine("Popping '{0}'", numbers.Pop());

    // Create a copy of the stack, using the ToArray method and the
    // constructor that accepts an IEnumerable<T>.
    Stack<string> stack2 = new Stack<string>(numbers.ToArray());

    Console.WriteLine("\nContents of the first copy:");
    foreach( string number in stack2 )
    {
      Console.WriteLine(number);
    }

    // Create an array twice the size of the stack and copy the
    // elements of the stack, starting at the middle of the
    // array.
    string[] array2 = new string[numbers.Count * 2];
    numbers.CopyTo(array2, numbers.Count);

    // Create a second stack, using the constructor that accepts an
    // IEnumerable(Of T).
    Stack<string> stack3 = new Stack<string>(array2);

    Console.WriteLine("\nContents of the second copy, with duplicates and nulls:");
    foreach( string number in stack3 )
```

```
   {
      Console.WriteLine(number);
   }

   Console.WriteLine("\nstack2.Contains(\"four\") = {0}",
      stack2.Contains("four"));

   Console.WriteLine("\nstack2.Clear()");
   stack2.Clear();
   Console.WriteLine("\nstack2.Count = {0}", stack2.Count);
   }
}
```

/* This code example produces the following output:

five
four
three
two
one

Popping 'five'
Peek at next item to destack: four
Popping 'four'

Contents of the first copy:
one
two
three

Contents of the second copy, with duplicates and nulls:
one
two
three

stack2.Contains("four") = False

stack2.Clear()

stack2.Count = 0
*/

Methods

Name	Description
Clear	Removes all objects from the Stack<T>.
Contains	Determines whether an element is in the Stack<T>.
CopyTo	Copies the Stack<T> to an existing one-dimensional Array, starting at the specified array index.
Equals(Object)	Determines whether the specified Object is equal to the current Object. (Inherited from Object.)
Peek	Returns the object at the top of the Stack<T> without removing it.
Pop	Removes and returns the object at the top of the Stack<T>.
Push	Inserts an object at the top of the Stack<T>.
ToArray	Copies the Stack<T> to a new array.
ToString	Returns a String that represents the current Object. (Inherited from Object.)
TrimExcess	Sets the capacity to the actual number of elements in the Stack<T>, if that number is less than 90 percent of current capacity.

Properties

Name	Description
Count	Gets the number of elements contained in the Stack<T>.

❖ Generics Queue

Queues are useful for storing messages in the order they were received for sequential processing. Objects stored in a Queue<T> are inserted at one end and removed from the other.

The capacity of a Queue<T> is the number of elements the Queue<T> can hold. As elements are added to a Queue<T>, the capacity is automatically increased as required by reallocating the internal array. The capacity can be decreased by calling TrimExcess.

Queue<T> accepts null as a valid value for reference types and allows duplicate elements.

Example

The following code example demonstrates several methods of the Queue<T> generic class. The code example creates a queue of strings with default capacity and uses the Enqueue method to queue five strings. The elements of the queue are enumerated, which does not change the state of the queue. The Dequeue method is used to dequeue the first string. The Peek method is used to look at the next item in the queue, and then the Dequeue method is used to dequeue it.

The ToArray method is used to create an array and copy the queue elements to it, then the array is passed to the Queue<T> constructor that takes IEnumerable<T>, creating a copy of the queue. The elements of the copy are displayed.

An array twice the size of the queue is created, and the CopyTo method is used to copy the array elements beginning at the middle of the array. The Queue<T> constructor is used again to create a second copy of the queue containing three null elements at the beginning.

The Contains method is used to show that the string "four" is in the first copy of the queue, after which the Clear method clears the copy and the Count property shows that the queue is empty.

```
using System;
using System.Collections.Generic;

class Example
{
   public static void Main()
   {
      Queue<string> numbers = new Queue<string>();
      numbers.Enqueue("one");
      numbers.Enqueue("two");
      numbers.Enqueue("three");
      numbers.Enqueue("four");
      numbers.Enqueue("five");

      // A queue can be enumerated without disturbing its contents.
      foreach( string number in numbers )
      {
         Console.WriteLine(number);
      }

      Console.WriteLine("\nDequeuing '{0}'", numbers.Dequeue());
      Console.WriteLine("Peek at next item to dequeue: {0}",
         numbers.Peek());
      Console.WriteLine("Dequeuing '{0}'", numbers.Dequeue());

      // Create a copy of the queue, using the ToArray method and the
      // constructor that accepts an IEnumerable<T>.
      Queue<string> queueCopy = new Queue<string>(numbers.ToArray());

      Console.WriteLine("\nContents of the first copy:");
      foreach( string number in queueCopy )
      {
         Console.WriteLine(number);
      }
```

```
// Create an array twice the size of the queue and copy the
// elements of the queue, starting at the middle of the
// array.
string[] array2 = new string[numbers.Count * 2];
numbers.CopyTo(array2, numbers.Count);

// Create a second queue, using the constructor that accepts an
// IEnumerable(Of T).
Queue<string> queueCopy2 = new Queue<string>(array2);

Console.WriteLine("\nContents of the second copy, with duplicates and nulls:");
foreach( string number in queueCopy2 )
{
    Console.WriteLine(number);
}

Console.WriteLine("\nqueueCopy.Contains(\"four\") = {0}",
    queueCopy.Contains("four"));

Console.WriteLine("\nqueueCopy.Clear()");
queueCopy.Clear();
Console.WriteLine("\nqueueCopy.Count = {0}", queueCopy.Count);
    }
}

/* This code example produces the following output:

one
two
three
four
five

Dequeuing 'one'
Peek at next item to dequeue: two
Dequeuing 'two'

Contents of the copy:
three
four
five

Contents of the second copy, with duplicates and nulls:

three
four
```

five

```
queueCopy.Contains("four") = True
queueCopy.Clear()
queueCopy.Count = 0
*/
```

Methods

Name	Description
Clear	Removes all objects from the Queue<T>.
Contains	Determines whether an element is in the Queue<T>.
CopyTo	Copies the Queue<T> elements to an existing one-dimensional Array, starting at the specified array index.
Dequeue	Removes and returns the object at the beginning of the Queue<T>.
Enqueue	Adds an object to the end of the Queue<T>.
Equals(Object)	Determines whether the specified Object is equal to the current Object. (Inherited from Object.)
Peek	Returns the object at the beginning of the Queue<T> without removing it.
ToArray	Copies the Queue<T> elements to a new array.
ToString	Returns a String that represents the current Object. (Inherited from Object.)
TrimExcess	Sets the capacity to the actual number of elements in the Queue<T>, if that number is less than 90 percent of current capacity.

Properties

Name	Description
Count	Gets the number of elements contained in the Queue<T>.

❖ Generics HashSet

The HashSet<T> class provides high performance set operations. A set is a collection that contains no duplicate elements, and whose elements are in no particular order.

The capacity of a HashSet<T> object is the number of elements that the object can hold. A HashSet<T> object's capacity automatically increases as elements are added to the object.

Starting with the .NET Framework version 4, the HashSet<T> class implements the ISet<T> interface.

```
using System;
using System.Collections.Generic;
using System.Linq;
```

```
class Program
{
  static void Main()
  {
    // Input array that contains three duplicate strings.
    string[] array1 = { "cat", "dog", "cat", "leopard", "tiger", "cat" };

    // Display the array.
    Console.WriteLine(string.Join(",", array1));

    // Use HashSet constructor to ensure unique strings.
    var hash = new HashSet<string>(array1);

    // Convert to array of strings again.
    string[] array2 = hash.ToArray();

    // Display the resulting array.
    Console.WriteLine(string.Join(",", array2));
  }
}
```

=== **Output of the program** ===

cat,dog,cat,leopard,tiger,cat
cat,dog,leopard,tiger

Methods

Name	Description
Add	Adds the specified element to a set.
Clear	Removes all elements from a HashSet<T> object.
Contains	Determines whether a HashSet<T> object contains the specified element.
CopyTo(T[])	Copies the elements of a HashSet<T> object to an array.
CopyTo(T[], Int32)	Copies the elements of a HashSet<T> object to an array, starting at the specified array index.
CopyTo(T[], Int32, Int32)	Copies the specified number of elements of a HashSet<T> object to an array, starting at the specified array index.
CreateSetComparer	Returns an IEqualityComparer object that can be used for equality testing of a HashSet<T> object.
Equals(Object)	Determines whether the specified Object is equal to the current Object. (Inherited from Object.)
ExceptWith	Removes all elements in the specified collection from the current HashSet<T> object.

Finalize	Allows an Object to attempt to free resources and perform other cleanup operations before the Object is reclaimed by garbage collection. (Inherited from Object.)
GetEnumerator	Returns an enumerator that iterates through a HashSet<T> object.
GetHashCode	Serves as a hash function for a particular type. (Inherited from Object.)
GetObjectData	Implements the System.Runtime.Serialization.ISerializable interface and returns the data needed to serialize a HashSet<T> object.
GetType	Gets the Type of the current instance. (Inherited from Object.)
IntersectWith	Modifies the current HashSet<T> object to contain only elements that are present in that object and in the specified collection.
IsProperSubsetOf	Determines whether a HashSet<T> object is a proper subset of the specified collection.
IsProperSupersetOf	Determines whether a HashSet<T> object is a proper superset of the specified collection.
IsSubsetOf	Determines whether a HashSet<T> object is a subset of the specified collection.
IsSupersetOf	Determines whether a HashSet<T> object is a superset of the specified collection.
MemberwiseClone	Creates a shallow copy of the current Object. (Inherited from Object.)
OnDeserialization	Implements the System.Runtime.Serialization.ISerializable interface and raises the deserialization event when the deserialization is complete.
Overlaps	Determines whether the current HashSet<T> object and a specified collection share common elements.
Remove	Removes the specified element from a HashSet<T> object.
RemoveWhere	Removes all elements that match the conditions defined by the specified predicate from a HashSet<T> collection.
SetEquals	Determines whether a HashSet<T> object and the specified collection contain the same elements.
SymmetricExceptWith	Modifies the current HashSet<T> object to contain only elements that are present either in that object or in the specified collection, but not both.
ToString	Returns a String that represents the current Object. (Inherited from Object.)
TrimExcess	Sets the capacity of a HashSet<T> object to the actual number of elements it contains, rounded up to a nearby, implementation-specific value.
UnionWith	Modifies the current HashSet<T> object to contain all elements that are present in both itself and in the specified collection.

Properties

Name	Description
Comparer	Gets the IEqualityComparer<T> object that is used to determine equality for the values in the set.
Count	Gets the number of elements that are contained in a set.

Chapter 7: Reflection in C#

❖ Attributes

An *attribute* is an object that represents data you want to associate with an element in your program. The element to which you attach an attribute is referred to as the *target* of that attribute. For example, the attribute:

[NoIDispatch]

is associated with a class or an interface to indicate that the target class should derive from IUnknown rather than IDispatch, when exporting to COM.

[assembly: AssemblyKeyFile("c:\myStrongName.key")]

This inserts metadata into the assembly to designate the program's StrongName.

➤ Intrinsic Attributes

Attributes come in two flavors: *intrinsic* and *custom*. Intrinsic attributes are supplied as part of the Common Language Runtime (CLR), and they are integrated into .NET. *Custom* attributes are attributes you create for your own purposes.

Most programmers will use only intrinsic attributes, though custom attributes can be a powerful tool when combined with reflection, described later in this chapter.

Attribute Targets

If you search through the CLR, you'll find a great many attributes. Some attributes are applied to an assembly, others to a class or interface, and some, such as [WebMethod], to class members. These are called the *attribute targets*. Possible attribute targets are detailed in Table.

Member Name	Usage
All	Applied to any of the following elements: assembly, class, class member, delegate, enum, event, field, interface, method, module, parameter, property, return value, or struct
Assembly	Applied to the assembly itself
Class	Applied to instances of the class
ClassMembers	Applied to classes, structs, enums, constructors, methods, properties, fields, events, delegates, and interfaces
Constructor	Applied to a given constructor
Delegate	Applied to the delegated method

Enum	Applied to an enumeration
Event	Applied to an event
Field	Applied to a field
Interface	Applied to an interface
Method	Applied to a method
Module	Applied to a single module
Parameter	Applied to a parameter of a method
Property	Applied to a property (both get and set, if implemented)
ReturnValue	Applied to a return value
Struct	Applied to a struct

Applying Attributes

You apply attributes to their targets by placing them in square brackets immediately before the target item. You can combine attributes, either by stacking one on top of another:

    [assembly: AssemblyDelaySign(false)]
    [assembly: AssemblyKeyFile(".\\keyFile.snk")] or by separating the attributes with
    commas:
    [assembly: AssemblyDelaySign(false), assembly: AssemblyKeyFile(".\\keyFile.snk")]

The System.Runtime namespace offers a number of intrinsic attributes, including attributes for assemblies (such as the keyname attribute), for configuration (such as debug to indicate the debug build), and for version attributes.

You can organize the intrinsic attributes by how they are used. The principal intrinsic attributes are those used for COM, those used to modify the Interface Definition Language (IDL) file from within a source-code file, attributes used by the ATL Server classes, and attributes used by the Visual C++ compiler.

Perhaps the attribute you are most likely to use in your everyday C# programming (if you are not interacting with COM) is [Serializable]. As you'll see in Chapter 19, all you need to do to ensure that your class can be serialized to disk or to the Internet is add the [Serializable] attribute to the class:

    [serializable]
    class MySerializableClass

The attribute tag is put in square brackets immediately before its target--in this case, the class declaration.

C# Programming Made Easy

The key fact about intrinsic attributes is that you know when you need them; the task will dictate their use.

➢ **Custom Attributes**

You are free to create your own custom attributes and use them at runtime as you see fit. Suppose, for example, that your development organization wants to keep track of bug fixes. You already keep a database of all your bugs, but you'd like to tie your bug reports to specific fixes in the code.

You might add comments to your code along the lines of:
// Bug 323 fixed by Jesse Liberty 1/1/2005.

This would make it easy to see in your source code, but there is no enforced connection to Bug 323 in the database. A custom attribute might be just what you need. You would replace your comment with something like this:

```
[BugFixAttribute(323,"Jesse Liberty","1/1/2005")
Comment="Off by one error"]
```

You could then write a program to read through the metadata to find these bug-fix notations and update the database. The attribute would serve the purposes of a comment, but would also allow you to retrieve the information programmatically through tools you'd create.

Declaring an Attribute

Attributes, like most things in C#, are embodied in classes. To create a custom attribute, you derive your new custom attribute class from System.Attribute:

public class BugFixAttribute : System.Attribute
You need to tell the compiler with which kinds of elements this attribute can be used (the attribute target). You specify this with (what else?) an attribute:

```
[AttributeUsage(AttributeTargets.Class |
  AttributeTargets.Constructor |
  AttributeTargets.Field |
  AttributeTargets.Method |
  AttributeTargets.Property,
  AllowMultiple = true)]
```

AttributeUsage is an attribute applied to attributes: a meta-attribute. It provides, if you will, meta-metadata -- that is, data about the metadata. For the AttributeUsage attribute constructor, you pass two arguments. The first argument is a set of flags that indicate the target -- in this case, the class and its constructor, fields, methods, and properties. The second argument is a flag that indicates whether a given element might receive more than one such attribute. In this example, AllowMultiple is set to true, indicating that class members can have more than one BugFixAttribute assigned.

Naming an Attribute

The new custom attribute in this example is named BugFixAttribute. The convention is to append the word Attribute to your attribute name. The compiler supports this by allowing you to call the attribute with the shorter version of the name. Thus, you can write:
[BugFix(123, "Jesse Liberty", "01/01/05", Comment="Off by one")]

The compiler will first look for an attribute named BugFix and, if it does not find that, will then look for BugFixAttribute.

Constructing an Attribute

Every attribute must have at least one constructor. Attributes take two types of parameters, *positional* and *named*. In the BugFix example, the programmer's name and the date are positional parameters, and comment is a named parameter. Positional parameters are passed in through the constructor and must be passed in the order declared in the constructor:

```
public BugFixAttribute(int bugID, string programmer,string date)
{
   this.bugID = bugID;
   this.programmer = programmer;
   this.date = date;
}
```

Named parameters are implemented as properties:

```
public string Comment
{
   get
   {
      return comment;
   }
   set
   {
      comment = value;
   }
}
```
It is common to create read-only properties for the positional parameters:
```
public int BugID
{
   get
   {
      return bugID;
   }
}
```

C# Programming Made Easy

Once you have defined an attribute, you can put it to work by placing it immediately before its target. To test the BugFixAttribute of the preceding example, the following program creates a simple class named MyMath and gives it two functions. You'll assign BugFixAttributes to the class to record its code-maintenance history:

```
[BugFixAttribute(121,"Jesse Liberty","01/03/05")]
[BugFixAttribute(107,"Jesse Liberty","01/04/05", Comment="Fixed off by one errors")]
public class MyMath
```

These attributes will be stored with the metadata. Example 18-1 shows the complete program.

Example

```
namespace Programming_CSharp
{
  using System;
  using System.Reflection;

  // create custom attribute to be assigned to class members
  [AttributeUsage(AttributeTargets.Class |
    AttributeTargets.Constructor |
    AttributeTargets.Field |
    AttributeTargets.Method |
    AttributeTargets.Property,
    AllowMultiple = true)]
  public class BugFixAttribute : System.Attribute
  {
    // attribute constructor for
    // positional parameters
    public BugFixAttribute
      (int bugID,
      string programmer,
      string date)
    {
      this.bugID = bugID;
      this.programmer = programmer;
      this.date = date;
    }

    // accessor
    public int BugID
    {
      get
      {
```

```
   return bugID;
  }
 }

 // property for named parameter
 public string Comment
 {
  get
  {
   return comment;
  }
  set
  {
   comment = value;
  }
 }

 // accessor
 public string Date
 {
  get
  {
   return date;
  }
 }

 // accessor
 public string Programmer
 {
  get
  {
   return programmer;
  }
 }
 // private member data
 private int   bugID;
 private string comment;
 private string date;
 private string programmer;
}

// ********* assign the attributes to the class ********

[BugFixAttribute(121,"Jesse Liberty","01/03/05")]
[BugFixAttribute(107,"Jesse Liberty","01/04/05",
  Comment="Fixed off by one errors")]
```

```
public class MyMath
{
 public double DoFunc1(double param1)
 {
   return param1 + DoFunc2(param1);
 }

 public double DoFunc2(double param1)
 {
   return param1 / 3;
 }
}

public class Tester
{
 public static void Main( )
 {
  MyMath mm = new MyMath( );
  Console.WriteLine("Calling DoFunc(7). Result: {0}",
    mm.DoFunc1(7));
 }
}
}
```

Output:
    Calling DoFunc(7). Result: 9.3333333333333339

❖ Reflection

For the attributes in the metadata to be useful, you need a way to access them -- ideally during runtime. The classes in the Reflection namespace, along with the System.Type and System.TypedReference classes, provide support for examining and interacting with the metadata.

Reflection is generally used for any of four tasks:

Viewing metadata
    This might be used by tools and utilities that wish to display metadata.
Performing type discovery
    This allows you to examine the types in an assembly and interact with or instantiate those types. This can be useful in creating custom scripts. For example, you might want to allow your users to interact with your program using a script language, such as JavaScript, or a scripting language you create yourself.
Late binding to methods and properties
    This allows the programmer to invoke properties and methods on objects dynamically instantiated based on type discovery. This is also known as *dynamic invocation*.

Creating types at runtime (Reflection Emit)

The ultimate use of reflection is to create new types at runtime and then to use those types to perform tasks. You might do this when a custom class, created at runtime, will run significantly faster than more generic code created at compile time. An example is offered later in this chapter.

Viewing MetaData

In this section, you will use the C# Reflection support to read the metadata in the MyMath class. You start by initializing an object of the type MemberInfo. This object, in the System.Reflection namespace, is provided to discover the attributes of a member and to provide access to the metadata:

System.Reflection.MemberInfo inf = typeof(MyMath);

You call the typeof operator on the MyMath type, which returns an object of type Type, which derives from MemberInfo.
The next step is to call GetCustomAttributes on this MemberInfo object, passing in the type of the attribute you want to find. What you get back is an array of objects, each of type BugFixAttribute:

object[] attributes;
attributes = inf.GetCustomAttributes(typeof(BugFixAttribute),false);

You can now iterate through this array, printing out the properties of the BugFixAttribute object.

Using Reflection

```
public static void Main( )
{
  MyMath mm = new MyMath( );
  Console.WriteLine("Calling DoFunc(7). Result: {0}",
    mm.DoFunc1(7));

  // get the member information and use it to
  // retrieve the custom attributes
  System.Reflection.MemberInfo inf = typeof(MyMath);
  object[] attributes;
  attributes =
    inf.GetCustomAttributes(
      typeof(BugFixAttribute), false);

  // iterate through the attributes, retrieving the
  // properties
  foreach(Object attribute in attributes)
  {
    BugFixAttribute bfa = (BugFixAttribute) attribute;
```

```
Console.WriteLine("\nBugID: {0}", bfa.BugID);
Console.WriteLine("Programmer: {0}", bfa.Programmer);
Console.WriteLine("Date: {0}", bfa.Date);
Console.WriteLine("Comment: {0}", bfa.Comment);
 }
}
```

Output:
Calling DoFunc(7). Result: 9.3333333333333339
BugID: 121
Programmer: Jesse Liberty
Date: 01/03/05
Comment:

BugID: 107
Programmer: Jesse Liberty
Date: 01/04/05
Comment: Fixed off by one errors

When you put this replacement code into Example 18-1 and run it, you can see the metadata printed as you'd expect.

Type Discovery

You can use reflection to explore and examine the contents of an assembly. You can find the types associated with a module; the methods, fields, properties, and events associated with a type, as well as the signatures of each of the type's methods; the interfaces supported by the type; and the type's base class.

To start, load an assembly dynamically with the Assembly.Load static method. The Assembly class encapsulates the actual assembly itself, for purposes of reflection. The signature for the Load method is:

    public static Assembly.Load(AssemblyName)

For the next example, pass in the Core Library to the Load method. MsCorLib.dll has the core classes of the .NET Framework:

    Assembly a = Assembly.Load("Mscorlib.dll");

Once the assembly is loaded, you can call GetTypes( ) to return an array of Type objects. The Type object is the heart of reflection. Type represents type declarations: classes, interfaces, arrays, values, and enumerations:

    Type[] types = a.GetTypes( );

The assembly returns an array of types that you can display in a foreach loop, as shown in Example 18-3. Because this listing uses the Type class, you will want to add a using statement for the System.Reflection namespace.

Reflecting on an assembly

```
namespace Programming_CSharp
{
  using System;
  using System.Reflection;

  public class Tester
  {
    public static void Main( )
    {
      // what is in the assembly
      Assembly a = Assembly.Load("Mscorlib.dll");
      Type[] types = a.GetTypes( );
      foreach(Type t in types)
      {
        Console.WriteLine("Type is {0}", t);
      }
      Console.WriteLine(
        "{0} types found", types.Length);
    }
  }
}
```

The output from this would fill many pages. Here is a short excerpt:
Type is System.TypeCode
Type is System.Security.Util.StringExpressionSet
Type is System.Runtime.InteropServices.COMException
Type is System.Runtime.InteropServices.SEHException
Type is System.Reflection.TargetParameterCountException
Type is System.Text.UTF7Encoding
Type is System.Text.UTF7Encoding$Decoder
Type is System.Text.UTF7Encoding$Encoder
Type is System.ArgIterator
Type is System.Runtime.Remoting.JITLookupTable
Type is System.Runtime.Remoting.IComponentServices
Type is System.Runtime.Remoting.ComponentServices
1429 types found

This example obtained an array filled with the types from the Core Library and printed them one by one. The array contained 1,429 entries on my machine.

C# Programming Made Easy

You can reflect on a single type in the mscorlib assembly as well. To do so, you extract a type from the assembly with the GetType( ) method.

Example

```
namespace Programming_CSharp
{
  using System;
  using System.Reflection;

  public class Tester
  {
    public static void Main( )
    {
      // examine a single object
      Type theType =
      Type.GetType(
        "System.Reflection.Assembly");
      Console.WriteLine(
        "\nSingle Type is {0}\n", theType);
    }
  }
}
```
Output:
Single Type is System.Reflection.Assembly

Finding all type members

You can ask the Assembly type for all its members using the GetMembers( ) method of the Type class, which lists all the methods, properties, and fields, as shown in Example 18-5.

Reflecting on the members of a type

```
namespace Programming_CSharp
{
  using System;
  using System.Reflection;

  public class Tester
  {
  public static void Main( )
  {
    // examine a single object
    Type theType =
    Type.GetType(
```

```
"System.Reflection.Assembly");
Console.WriteLine(
"\nSingle Type is {0}\n", theType);

// get all the members
MemberInfo[] mbrInfoArray =
theType.GetMembers( );
foreach (MemberInfo mbrInfo in mbrInfoArray )
{
  Console.WriteLine("{0} is a {1}",
    mbrInfo, mbrInfo.MemberType);
  }
 }
 }
}
```

Once again the output is quite lengthy, but within the output you see fields, methods, constructors, and properties, as shown in this excerpt:

```
System.String s_localFilePrefix is a Field
Boolean IsDefined(System.Type) is a Method
Void .ctor( ) is a Constructor
System.String CodeBase  is a Property
System.String CopiedCodeBase  is a Property
```

Finding type methods

You might want to focus on methods only, excluding the fields, properties, and so forth. To do so, you remove the call to GetMembers( ):

```
        MemberInfo[] mbrInfoArray =
        theType.GetMembers(BindingFlags.LookupAll);
        and add a call to GetMethods( ):
        mbrInfoArray = theType.GetMethods( );
```

The output now is nothing but the methods:

Output (excerpt):

```
Boolean Equals(System.Object) is a Method
System.String ToString( ) is a Method
System.String CreateQualifiedName(System.String, System.String) is a Method
System.Reflection.MethodInfo get_EntryPoint( ) is a Method
```

C# Programming Made Easy

Finding particular type members

Finally, to narrow it down even further, you can use the FindMembers method to find particular members of the type. For example, you can narrow your search to methods whose names begin with the letters Get.

To narrow the search, you use the FindMembers method, which takes four parameters: MemberTypes, BindingFlags, MemberFilter, and object.

MemberTypes

A MemberTypes object that indicates the type of the member to search for. These include All, Constructor, Custom, Event, Field, Method, Nestedtype, Property, and TypeInfo. You will also use the MemberTypes.Method to find a method.

BindingFlags

An enumeration that controls the way searches are conducted by reflection. There are a great many BindingFlag values, including IgnoreCase, Instance, Public, Static, and so forth. The BindingFlags default member indicates no binding flag, which is what you want because you do not want to restrict the binding.

MemberFilter

A delegate (see Chapter 12) that is used to filter the list of members in the MemberInfo array of objects. The filter you'll use is Type.FilterName, a field of the Type class used for filtering on a name.

Object

A string value that will be used by the filter. In this case you'll pass in "Get*" to match only those methods that begin with the letters Get.

The complete listing for filtering on these methods is shown in Example 18-6.

Finding particular members

```
namespace Programming_CSharp
{
 using System;
 using System.Reflection;

 public class Tester
 {
 public static void Main( )
 {
  // examine a single object
  Type theType = Type.GetType(
  "System.Reflection.Assembly");

  // just members which are methods beginning with Get
  MemberInfo[] mbrInfoArray =
  theType.FindMembers(MemberTypes.Method,
   BindingFlags.Default,
   Type.FilterName, "Get*");
  foreach (MemberInfo mbrInfo in mbrInfoArray )
```

```
{
  Console.WriteLine("{0} is a {1}",
    mbrInfo, mbrInfo.MemberType);
  }
 }
}
```

Output (excerpt):
System.Type[] GetTypes( ) is a Method
System.Type[] GetExportedTypes( ) is a Method
System.Type GetType(System.String, Boolean) is a Method
System.Type GetType(System.String) is a Method
System.Reflection.AssemblyName GetName(Boolean) is a Method
System.Reflection.AssemblyName GetName( ) is a Method
Int32 GetHashCode( ) is a Method

Dynamic Loading (Late Binding)

Once you have discovered a method, it's possible to invoke it using reflection. For example, you might like to invoke the Cos( ) method of System.Math, which returns the cosine of an angle. To invoke Cos( ), you will first get the Type information for the System.Math class:
Type theMathType = Type.GetType("System.Math");
With that type information, you can dynamically load an instance of that class by using a static method of the Activator class.
The Activator class contains four methods, all static, which you can use to create objects locally or remotely or to obtain references to existing objects. The four methods are: CreateComInstanceFrom, CreateInstanceFrom, GetObject, and CreateInstance:

CreateComInstanceFrom
    Used to create instances of COM objects.
CreateInstanceFrom
    Used to create a reference to an object from a particular assembly and type name.
GetObject
    Used when marshaling objects. Marshaling is discussed in detail in Chapter 19.
CreateInstance
    Used to create local or remote instances of an object. You'll use this method to instantiate   an   object   of   the   System.Math   class.
    Object theObj = Activator.CreateInstance(theMathType);

You now have two objects in hand: a Type object named TheMathType, which you created by calling GetType, and an instance of the System.Math class named theObj, which you instantiated by calling CreateInstance.
Before you can invoke a method on the object, you must get the method you need from the Type object, theMathType. To do so, you'll call GetMethod(), and you'll pass in the signature of the Cos method.

C# Programming Made Easy

The signature, you will remember, is the name of the method (Cos) and its parameter types. In the case of Cos(), there is only one parameter: a double. Whereas, Type.GetMethod takes two parameters: the first represents the name of the method you want, and the second represents the parameters. The name is passed as a string; the parameters are passed as an array of types:

MethodInfo CosineInfo = theMathType.GetMethod("Cos",paramTypes);

Before calling GetMethod, you must prepare the array of types:
    Type[] paramTypes = new Type[1];
    paramTypes[0]= Type.GetType("System.Double");

This code declares the array of Type objects and then fills the first element (paramTypes[0]) with a Type representing a double. You obtain that type representing a double by calling the static method Type.GetType(), passing in the string System.Double.

You now have an object of type MethodInfo on which you can invoke the method. To do so, you must pass in the actual value of the parameters, again in an array:

    Object[] parameters = new Object[1];
    parameters[0] = 45;
    Object returnVal = CosineInfo.Invoke(theObj,parameters);
    Type[] paramTypes = new Type[0];

Odd as this looks, it is correct.

Dynamically invoking a method

```
namespace Programming_CSharp
{
 using System;
 using System.Reflection;

 public class Tester
 {
 public static void Main( )
 {
   Type theMathType = Type.GetType("System.Math");
   Object theObj =
   Activator.CreateInstance(theMathType);

   // array with one member
   Type[] paramTypes = new Type[1];
   paramTypes[0]= Type.GetType("System.Double");

   // Get method info for Cos( )
   MethodInfo CosineInfo =
   theMathType.GetMethod("Cos",paramTypes);
```

```
// fill an array with the actual parameters
Object[] parameters = new Object[1];
parameters[0] = 45;
Object returnVal =
CosineInfo.Invoke(theObj,parameters);
Console.WriteLine(
"The cosine of a 45 degree angle {0}",
returnVal);

    }
   }
}
```

That was a lot of work just to invoke a single method. The power, however, is that you can use reflection to discover an assembly on the user's machine, use reflection to query what methods are available, and then use reflection to invoke one of those members dynamically!